D0936990

WITHDRAWN

JOHN F. KENNEDY

JOHN F. KENNEDY

A Biography

Michael Meagher and Larry D. Gragg

GREENWOOD BIOGRAPHIES

 GREENWOOD

AN IMPRINT OF ABC-CLIO, LLC
Santa Barbara, California • Denver, Colorado • Oxford, England

Copyright 2011 by Michael Meagher and Larry D. Gragg

All rights reserved. No part of this publication may be reproduced, stored in a retrieval system, or transmitted, in any form or by any means, electronic, mechanical, photocopying, recording, or otherwise, except for the inclusion of brief quotations in a review, without prior permission in writing from the publisher.

Library of Congress Cataloging-in-Publication Data

Meagher, Michael.
   John F. Kennedy : a biography / Michael Meagher and Larry D. Gragg.
      p. cm. — (Greenwood biographies)
   Includes bibliographical references and index.
   ISBN 978-0-313-35416-8 (hardcopy : alk. paper) — ISBN 978-0-313-35417-5
(ebook) 1. Kennedy, John F. (John Fitzgerald), 1917–1963. 2. Presidents—
United States—Biography. I. Gragg, Larry Dale, 1950– II. Title.
   E842.K43M43 2011
   973.922092—dc23
   [B]   2011017654

ISBN: 978-0-313-35416-8
EISBN: 978-0-313-35417-5

15 14 13 12 11   1 2 3 4 5

This book is also available on the World Wide Web as an eBook.
Visit www.abc-clio.com for details.

Greenwood
An Imprint of ABC-CLIO, LLC

ABC-CLIO, LLC
130 Cremona Drive, P.O. Box 1911
Santa Barbara, California 93116-1911

This book is printed on acid-free paper (∞)

Manufactured in the United States of America

CONTENTS

CONTENTS

SERIES FOREWORD

In response to high school and public library needs, Greenwood developed this distinguished series of full-length biographies specifically for student use. Prepared by field experts and professionals, these engaging biographies are tailored for high school students who need challenging yet accessible biographies. Ideal for secondary school assignments, the length, format and subject areas are designed to meet educators' requirements and students' interests.

Greenwood offers an extensive selection of biographies spanning all curriculum related subject areas including social studies, the sciences, literature and the arts, history and politics, as well as popular culture, covering public figures and famous personalities from all time periods and backgrounds, both historic and contemporary, who have made an impact on American and/or world culture. Greenwood biographies were chosen based on comprehensive feedback from librarians and educators. Consideration was given to both curriculum relevance and inherent interest. The result is an intriguing mix of the well known and the unexpected, the saints and sinners from long-ago history and contemporary pop culture. Readers will find a wide array of subject choices from fascinating crime figures like Al Capone to inspiring pioneers like Margaret Mead, from the greatest minds of our time like Stephen Hawking to the most amazing success stories of our day like J. K. Rowling.

While the emphasis is on fact, not glorification, the books are meant to be fun to read. Each volume provides in-depth information about the subject's life from birth through childhood, the teen years, and adulthood. A thorough account relates family background and education, traces personal and professional influences, and explores struggles, accomplishments, and contributions. A timeline highlights the most significant life events against a historical perspective. Bibliographies supplement the reference value of each volume.

INTRODUCTION

It is a beautiful sunny day in Dallas, Texas, on November 22, 1963. The city is hosting President John F. Kennedy and the First Lady. The president has had some misgivings about the Texas trip. In fact, his staff has urged him not to make it. Yet the visit is turning into a success as the young couple receives a warm welcome from the residents. Approaching 12:30 P.M., the president's motorcade makes its way through the downtown area of Dallas; members of the secret service are nervous, as the tall buildings pose a security risk to the nation's chief executive. There is a sigh of relief as the motorcade leaves Dealey Plaza and moves into a more open area. Members of the president's entourage feel that the danger is passed. Suddenly, shots ring out, and the president and Texas governor John Connally slump. In an instant comes the fatal shot to the president's head, and the "murder of the century" enters the history books.

In the days, months, and years following the Kennedy assassination, competing visions of the president's legacy emerged. Commentators offered profuse praise in newspaper and magazine articles in the immediate aftermath of his death. Led by distinguished historian and former presidential aide Arthur M. Schlesinger Jr., several authors crafted a "Camelot" image of Kennedy's administration in the wake of the tragedy. Besides Schlesinger's *A Thousand Days: John F. Kennedy in the White House* (1965) and William Manchester's best-selling *The Death of a President* (1967), several people close to Kennedy published recollections of their relationships with him. Key supporters Kenneth P. O'Donnell and David F. Powers published *"Johnny, We Hardly Knew Ye": Memories of John Fitzgerald Kennedy*; his longtime secretary Evelyn Lincoln released *My Twelve Years with John F. Kennedy*; and Kennedy's mother, Rose Fitzgerald Kennedy, published her autobiography entitled *Times to Remember*, all between 1965 and 1974. The image that emerges from these pages is one of a young, vigorous president leading the nation through international tension and inspiring idealism at home. Although Kennedy was in office for a short time, these authors portrayed him as an idealistic president who compared favorably with his Democratic predecessors Franklin D. Roosevelt and Harry S. Truman. The promoters of the Camelot image saw the Kennedy years as a special time in which art, culture, sophistication, and public service were hallmarks of the administration. For some it was a return to the romance and glamour of the court of the mythical King Arthur as depicted in a popular Broadway play called *Camelot*, which opened in 1960. Those who wrote about Kennedy in these terms cultivated this image so successfully that it remained the dominant interpretation of the Kennedy legacy through the early 1970s.

Yet beneath the surface of this imagery were some competing realities. Rather than an idealist, Kennedy was an extremely successful practical politician. He was a rational man who did not care for what he at one time called the emotional liberals. Political scientist James MacGregor Burns, for example, questioned Kennedy's ability to commit to moral questions, such as civil rights. He wrote a book about Kennedy for the 1960 presidential campaign, and the family was unhappy with the book. Burns later consented to an oral history interview with the Kennedy Library in which he called Jack's approach to politics "operationalism," which is an approach to politics that is centered on making deals. Burns claimed this caused Jack to miss out on chances to exercise moral leadership. "The more you do this, the more you may blur the great national debating grounds. The result is to enhance deals, bargains, operationalism in politics, and divest it of moral commitment."[1]

Another interpretation of the Kennedy years developed in the 1970s and became ever more critical of the Kennedy legacy as the years passed by. The new interpretation not only offered a critical evaluation of Kennedy's accomplishments but also explored Kennedy's personal life. Henry Fairlie's *The Kennedy Promise: The Politics of Expectation* (1973) claimed that Kennedy was all style and that he lacked substance. The Kennedy legacy comprised hollow words and appearances, according to Fairlie, and the idealism was false. Other writers used harsher words to bring down the image of Camelot, detailing the president's extra-marital affairs, efforts to hide the seriousness of his health problems, and the unsavory connections between the Kennedys and organized crime. Thomas Reeves's *A Question of Character: A Life of John F. Kennedy* (1991), for example, suggested that Kennedy lacked a moral center and that the president's womanizing revealed a reckless streak.

Sorting out these contradictory images must begin with a look at the story of the Kennedy family in America, which is a tale of remarkable achievement.

NOTE

1. James MacGregor Burns, interview by William H. Brubeck, May 14, 1965, John F. Kennedy Oral History Program, John F. Kennedy Library and Museum.

TIMELINE: EVENTS IN THE LIFE OF JOHN F. KENNEDY

May 29, 1917	John Fitzgerald Kennedy is born in Brookline, Massachusetts, the son of Patrick Joseph and Rose Fitzgerald Kennedy.
October 2, 1931	Enters Choate boarding school in Wallingford, Connecticut.
November 1935	Admitted to Princeton University, but leaves the university in December due to illness.
July 1936	After recuperating in Florida and Arizona, admitted to Harvard University.
Summer 1937	Travels in Europe with friend Lemoyne Billings.
1940	Publishes *Why England Slept*, his senior thesis at Harvard. The study of England's unpreparedness for war becomes a bestseller.
June 1940	Graduates from Harvard University and is accepted at Stanford University School of Business Administration.
October 1940	Registers for the draft.
September 1941	Commissioned as an ensign in the U.S. Navy.

August 2, 1943	Commands crew of PT 109, which sinks in sea battle in the South Pacific. Leads surviving crew members to safety and rescue.
August 12, 1944	Brother Joseph Kennedy Jr., aviator, killed when his plane explodes over English Channel.
1945	Works as journalist for Hearst newspapers covering the UN Conference in San Francisco, the English elections, and Potsdam Conference.
June 18, 1946	Wins Democratic primary for the Eleventh Congressional District in Massachusetts.
November 5, 1946	Wins election to the U.S. House of Representatives for the Eleventh Congressional District in Massachusetts with more than 70 percent of the vote.
January 14, 1947	Junior Chamber of Commerce names Kennedy one of the 10 outstanding young men of the year.
Fall 1947	Diagnosed with Addison's disease while on a trip to England.
November 2, 1948	Wins reelection to the U.S. House of Representatives for the Eleventh Congressional District in Massachusetts.
November 7, 1950	Wins reelection to the U.S. House of Representatives for the Eleventh Congressional District in Massachusetts.
1951	Takes extensive foreign trips to Europe, the Middle East, and Asia.
December 1951	First of many appearances on NBC program *Meet the Press*.
November 4, 1952	Wins election to the U.S. Senate defeating incumbent Republican Henry Cabot Lodge.
September 12, 1953	Marries Jacqueline Bouvier in Newport, Rhode Island.
October 30, 1953	Appears on Edward R. Murrow's *Person to Person* program with wife Jackie.

October 21, 1954	Has back surgery in New York, develops an infection, slips into a coma, and is given the last rites of the Catholic Church. Recovery from the surgery takes several months.
December 2, 1954	Because he remains in a hospital, he is not available to join other senators to vote on the censure of Senator Joseph McCarthy for his excesses in anticommunist crusade.
January 1956	Publishes *Profiles in Courage*, which becomes a bestseller and wins the Pulitzer Prize for biography in 1957.
August 13–17, 1956	At the Democratic Convention delivers nominating speech for Adlai Stevenson and narrowly loses the nomination for vice president to Estes Kefauver.
Fall 1956	Campaigns extensively for the Stevenson-Kefauver ticket.
1957	Serves on the McClellan Rackets Committee and the Foreign Relations Committee.
November 27, 1957	First child, Caroline, is born.
November 4, 1958	Wins reelection to the U.S. Senate.
January 2, 1960	Announces his candidacy for the presidential nomination.
May 10, 1960	Wins critical West Virginia primary defeating chief rival Senator Hubert H. Humphrey of Minnesota.
July 11–15, 1960	Wins nomination for president at the Democratic Convention. Selects Texas Senator Lyndon B. Johnson as his running mate.
September 26, 1960	Participates in first of four debates with Republican nominee Richard Nixon.
November 8, 1960	Wins the presidential election by fewer than 120,000 popular votes, but wins 303 electoral votes to 219 for Richard Nixon.
November 25, 1960	Second child, John Jr., is born.
January 20, 1961	Inaugurated as the 35th president of the United States.

April 14–19, 1961	U.S.-backed Cuban rebels lead a failed invasion of their homeland at the Bay of Pigs.
May 25, 1961	Announces a space program goal of landing a man on the moon.
June 3–4, 1961	Attends U.S.-USSR Summit in Vienna, Austria, and meets with Nikita Khrushchev.
August 1961	Initiates the Alliance for Progress program of aid to Latin American nations.
August 13, 1961	Construction begins on the wall between East and West Berlin.
April 1962	Forces steel companies to roll back price increases.
October 14–28, 1962	Cuban Missile Crisis.
June 11, 1963	Gives speech calling civil rights struggle a "moral crisis" in America.
Summer 1963	Buddhist monks protest Ngo Dinh Diem government in South Vietnam.
August 7, 1963	Third child, Patrick, is born. Dies two days later.
October 7, 1963	United States, USSR, and Great Britain sign Test Ban Treaty, which prohibits nuclear weapons testing in the atmosphere, under water, or in outer space.
November 2, 1963	Ngo Dinh Diem, South Vietnamese president, assassinated.
November 22, 1963	Assassinated in Dallas, Texas.
November 24, 1963	Suspected assassin Lee Harvey Oswald murdered by Jack Ruby in Dallas.
November 25, 1963	Buried at Arlington National Cemetery.

Chapter 1

THE KENNEDY FAMILY: MODEST BEGINNINGS AND BEYOND

From the shrewd business acumen of Joseph Patrick Kennedy Sr. to the athletic prowess of his eldest son, Joe Jr., the Kennedys extolled the virtues of competition. Fierce rivalry among the children of Joe and Rose Kennedy was common, and even encouraged. In this environment, the future 35th president of the United States spent his childhood and adolescence. Yet Jack did not possess the typical Kennedy family attribute of strength. Often sick, he lacked the physical strength of his older brother. Unlike the other Kennedys, Jack found solace in reading. His interest in books and his poor health charted the young man's future path. Given his predilection for reading he was not viewed as someone who would pursue a career in politics. Jack's outlier status in the Kennedy clan remained a constant in his life. Denied good health, he pursued strength in other ways such as stretching the limits of his body in campaigning and governing, and in directing a vigorous foreign policy as president.

Both the paternal and maternal sides of Jack's family had strong ties to the Irish Catholic community of Boston and to the politics of the city. His father was the son of Patrick Joseph Kennedy (P.J.), the only son of Irish immigrants Patrick and Bridget Kennedy, who was a leading Democratic politician in Massachusetts. His mother, Rose, was the daughter of John "Honey Fitz" Fitzgerald, twice-elected mayor of Boston.

Possessing the Kennedy attributes of a healthy body and a strong work ethic, P. J. worked on the docks of Boston harbor. A thrifty young man, he saved a good portion of his earnings and purchased three bars, one of which was close to his old place of work, the docks; another in the Haymarket Square area of Boston; and a third for upper-class Bostonians in a hotel called the Maverick House. P. J. gradually involved himself in the local politics of the Irish enclave of Boston, and this led to a political career. In 1884, P. J. won election to the Massachusetts House of Representatives, and he served five one-year terms in that body. Beginning in 1894, he won a seat in the Massachusetts Senate and served three two-year terms. In the meantime, P. J. served as "boss" of an influential ward in Boston. He was a delegate to the Democratic National Convention in 1888 where he gave a speech in support of Grover Cleveland, the party's presidential nominee. He married Mary Augusta Hickey on November 23, 1887. They had three children, including Joseph Kennedy, the father of John F. Kennedy.

Ironically, P. J. Kennedy became embroiled in a political battle with the family of Rose Fitzgerald. Rose's father, Honey Fitz, the son of a businessman and a graduate of Boston College, won election to the Massachusetts Senate in 1892. After serving three terms in the U.S. House of Representatives, Fitzgerald ran as a reform candidate for mayor of Boston against the wishes of the political bosses, including P. J. Kennedy. Fitzgerald won the office in 1905 and again in 1910. In 1913, James Michael Curley had his sights upon the post of mayor. Curley, in alliance with many of Boston's Democratic Party leaders, including P. J. Kennedy, forced Fitzgerald to give up his bid for another term. In this regard, Fitzgerald may have been persuaded by Curley's hint that he might release information about the mayor's alleged extramarital affair.

The withdrawal of Honey Fitz from the race was fraught with intrigue and ugly accusations. Elizabeth Ryan ("Toodles") had revealed to her attorney that Honey Fitz had had a sexual affair with her. Political allies of Curley managed to gain access to this information, and aimed it directly at the Fitzgerald household. A letter arrived at the mayor's home detailing the affair, and both Rose and her mother,

Josie, were shocked at the revelations contained in it. An angry scene took place at the Fitzgerald home, with his wife and daughter hurling bitter words at the mayor. The mayor's wife insisted that he not seek reelection. Accordingly, on December 17, 1913, Honey Fitz announced that he would not seek reelection as Boston's mayor. James Michael Curley went on to win several terms as mayor and then as governor of Massachusetts.

The opposition of P. J. Kennedy to Honey Fitz's renomination seems to have had little impact on the budding relationship between Joe Kennedy and Rose Fitzgerald. Much to the chagrin of Honey Fitz, the two developed an attraction that ultimately caused Rose's father to resort to extreme measures to keep her away from Joe Kennedy. After attending Boston Latin School, Joe had gained admission to Harvard University in 1908, a great challenge for an Irishman in "Yankee"-dominated Boston society. As Joe's future wife Rose related, the tensions and divisions between the Yankees and Irish were sharp: "There were two societies in Boston. One of them was almost entirely Protestant and was mainly of English descent, though with admixtures of Scottish, Scot-Irish, and even some Irish, plus a soupcon of French and others; in any case, all descended from colonial or early American settlers, blended together into the general breed called Yankee or 'proper Bostonians'."[1] The other group included the more recent arrivals, the Irish. "Between the two groups feelings were, at best, suspicious, and in general amounted to a state of chronic, mutual antagonism," Rose said.[2] Nevertheless, Joe was involved in student government and gained a spot on the university's baseball team. However, he was not academically gifted and passed through Harvard with a mediocre record. Joe's struggles to fit in at Harvard fueled a hungry drive for success once he left the university.

In contrast, Rose Fitzgerald received her education in Catholic schools and abroad. She attended Sacred Heart Academy in Boston, with a concentration in the art of managing a household. In 1908, Rose's parents sent her to the Netherlands where she enrolled in a convent. Some of these moves, especially the ones taken abroad, were intended to keep Joe and Rose apart. Nevertheless, while in Boston, Rose met frequently with Joe, and despite the parents' opposition the romance grew. Finally, Honey Fitz relented, and on October 7, 1914, Rose and Joe were married, and the couple bought a house in Brookline, Massachusetts. Less than a year later, on July 15, 1915, their first child, Joseph Patrick Kennedy Jr., was born. On May 29, 1917, John Fitzgerald Kennedy was born.

As the Joe Kennedy household increased in its number of children, it also grew financially. Following his graduation from Harvard in 1912, Joe decided upon a career in banking, starting as a clerk in his father's bank, Columbia Trust. After serving as a bank examiner, Joe became the president of Columbia Trust at age 25. However, his major break came with the outbreak of World War I when he became the assistant manager of Bethlehem Steel's Quincy, Massachusetts, shipbuilding plant at $15,000 annually, a handsome sum for that time. Besides the excellent salary, the new job served another purpose. Taking this position, Kennedy biographer Michael O'Brien has explained, permitted Joe "to

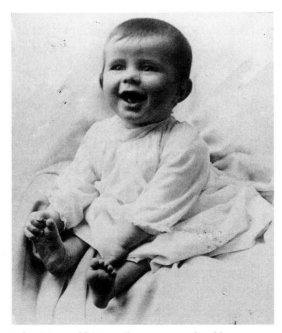

John Fitzgerald Kennedy at six months old, Brookline, MA, 1917. (AP Photo/John F. Kennedy National Historic Site)

avoid serving in the war."[3] Moreover, his position gave him the means and the opportunity to invest more aggressively. Over the next decade, Joe developed a reputation as a talented stockbroker, netting almost $2 million during the market boom of the Roaring Twenties. He also became involved in the rapidly growing movie industry in Hollywood. Like many producers of the time, Joe cared little about the artistic merits of movies. His prime consideration was profit. Joe's studios produced a large number of mediocre films, most of which served to enrich the pocket of the 35th president's father. As Prohibition was ending, Joe also invested in the liquor importation business. His company called Somerset Importers had the exclusive contract with several popular brands like Gordon's gin. Joe's insatiable appetite for money made him one of the richest men in America. He was able to provide each of his children with a trust fund that by 1949 had reached $10 million. The keen sense of competitiveness that characterized Joe at Harvard was ever more present in his conduct of business affairs, and the acquisition of power became a major pursuit in his life. He worked to instill these values in his children, especially in his oldest son Joe Jr.

At the same time that Joe was demonstrating his financial prowess on Wall Street and in the emerging movie industry of the United States, he remained steadfast in his loyalty to the Democratic Party. Like most Irish Americans, Joe enthusiastically supported the first Roman Catholic to secure a presidential nomination, Governor Al Smith of New York, who in 1928 became the Democratic Party's candidate for president. Joe and Roman Catholics throughout the nation were bitterly disappointed when Smith lost the election to the Republican Party nominee, Herbert Hoover. For the next 30 years, analysts and politicians cited Al Smith's defeat as proof that a Roman Catholic could not win the presidency. Joe himself had presidential ambitions, although his political missteps in the late 1930s as the U.S. ambassador to Great Britain ruined his chances to become president. Nevertheless, it became Joe's ever-present dream to elect a Catholic to the presidency, but not just any Roman Catholic. It was Joe's intent that his gifted eldest son Joe Jr. would become the first Catholic president of the United States. When Joe Jr.'s death in World War II precluded that possibility, the responsibility if not the burden of carrying forward Joe's dream came to rest on his overlooked second son, John Fitzgerald Kennedy.

NOTES

1. Rose Fitzgerald Kennedy, *Times to Remember* (Garden City, NY: Doubleday, 1974), p. 49.

2. Kennedy, *Times to Remember,* p. 50.

3. Michael O'Brien, *John Kennedy: A Biography* (New York: Thomas Dunne Books, 2005), p. 19.

Chapter 2

FROM STUDENT TO WAR HERO: JACK'S EARLY YEARS

At the beginning of her autobiography, Rose Kennedy makes a passing reference to her family's challenges and tragedies: "Now I am in my eighties, and I have known the joys and sorrows of a full life. Age, however, has its privileges. One is to reminisce and another is to reminisce selectively. I prefer to remember the good times, and that is how this book begins."[1] As a mother and wife, Rose experienced loss, betrayal, and the sense of being overwhelmed by having so many children. Many have criticized Rose's style of parenting, but her husband Joe was certainly not an ideal father either. Regardless of who was to blame, it is clear that John Fitzgerald Kennedy did not have a stable upbringing. To a large extent, Joe Kennedy was absent, amassing his fortune and running his various enterprises. Yet, this did not mean that Jack's mother, Rose, filled the gaps left by a very busy father. Rose had a distant personality, and she found it difficult to be emotionally demonstrative. Indeed, she once highlighted a magazine article that read, "Emotionalism in front of people is a great sign of immaturity."[2] Because she was aloof, Jack and his siblings did not receive much warmth from Rose. Indeed, although he was gone much of the time, Joe was the more affectionate parent. Rose managed a strict household with rules and procedures to be followed. These rules were especially difficult for Jack, and he often frustrated his mother when he expressed his individuality. Rose was frequently absent from home, routinely making trips to Europe; 17 trips in the 1930s alone. Rose especially loved Paris and traveled there often on shopping trips. A truly dedicated shopper, Rose purchased more than 200 dresses in 1940. Rose's natural affinity for Europe was understandable, as her father Honey Fitz had sent her there as a young lady where she attended a Catholic school with young women from prominent Catholic French and German families. Honey Fitz also frequently went to Europe and in 1911 had even sung "Sweet Adelaide," his trademark song, to Germany's last emperor, Kaiser Wilhelm II.

In all, Joe and Rose had nine children between 1915 and 1932: Joseph Jr., John, Rosemary, Kathleen, Eunice, Patricia, Robert, Jean, and Edward. Their children received little affection, and their parents reared them to be competitive. While order was important to Rose, this did not preclude lively activities by the children, especially athletics. Despite Jack's physical inferiority to his older brother Joe Jr., the boys were natural rivals. Jack was frequently on the losing side of these athletic contests and fights, but neither of his parents would have tolerated Jack's submission to his elder brother. Of all his siblings, Jack was probably closest to his sister Kathleen, nicknamed by the family as "Kick." Both Jack and Kick were more individualistic than their other siblings, and this certainly helped form a bond between the two. Jack was devastated by the tragic death of his sister in 1948.

It seems that almost from his infancy Jack was physically ill. According to Rose, who maintained an index card for each child with notations on their illnesses, "Jack was a healthy infant too, but then, as noted on his card: 'has had whooping cough, measles—chicken pox,' childhood diseases that were expectable in those days but that of course caused worries about him."[3] On February 20, 1920, Rose noted that Jack contracted a serious case of scarlet fever. In fact, he was so ill that he had to be hospitalized.

In 1927, Joe Kennedy moved his growing family to the New York City suburb of Riverdale and two years later to the suburb of

Bronxville. He did so, in part, because of his expanding business interests, but also because he believed Boston "was no place to bring up Irish Catholic children."[4] That same year, Joe met the young, attractive actress Gloria Swanson. This marked the beginnings of an affair that would have a pronounced impact on the Kennedy family, including the children, and on the relationship between Joe and Rose. Years earlier, Josie Fitzgerald, wife of Honey Fitz, had become exasperated over the impact that her husband's affair with "Toodles" Ryan would have on her daughter's entry into society. Now, Rose, who wanted so much to fit into society, had to face the challenge of her husband's infidelity in a city that did not include her longtime friends and extended family.

The relationship between Joe and Gloria Swanson became widely known. Joe even brought his lover into his home. Actually, this was not the first time that Joe had brought mistresses into the Kennedy home. Rose, who disdained shows of emotion, showed none when confronted with her husband's mistresses. However, Rose used the affair with Gloria Swanson to gain expensive jewelry and trips abroad. As biographer Nigel Hamilton explained, "To a neighbor Rose herself later confided that she made her husband 'pay' for his infidelity. 'I made him give me everything I wanted. Clothes, jewels, everything,' she remarked—oblivious to the cost to her children of her spite. 'Jack told a friend he used to cry every time she packed her bags until he realized that his crying irritated her to no end and only made her withdraw from him even more,' the family chronicler recorded."[5]

It is easy to look back at the Kennedy family photos and see the smiling faces and the attractive children, yet not realize that this was a dysfunctional family. The image and the reality were at odds. With both parents frequently away, and with Joe's intense drive for business success, as well as his infidelity, a picture emerges of children living in a world devoid of what Rose dismissively called "emotionalism." In the period following Jack's assassination, when rumors of his own infidelity became public knowledge, the information was rather shocking; Jack's image had been carefully crafted. His infidelity, however, should not have been surprising considering his father's actions while Jack was growing up.

The Kennedy family in the mid-1930s: Joseph P. Kennedy Sr. (center); from bottom left: Robert, Eunice, John, Kathleen, Joe Jr., Rosemary, Rose, Teddy, Patricia, and Jean. (AP Photo)

EDUCATION

Joe and Rose sent both Joe Jr. and Jack to upper-class boarding schools. Joe Jr. attended Choate, a private college preparatory institution for the children of the elite in Wallingford, Connecticut. Two future members of Jack's cabinet attended Choate, Chester Bowles and Adlai Stevenson. While at Choate, Joe Jr. compiled a strong academic and athletic record. After a year in a public school, Jack attended a series of exclusive private schools in Massachusetts, New York, and Connecticut. Rose and Joe had disagreements over the proper school for their second son. Rose prevailed in her preference for a Catholic education for Jack. While at Canterbury School in New Milford, Connecticut, Jack struggled with Latin, a subject that remained a mystery to him throughout his years in preparatory school. Indeed, he had to retake the Latin entrance exam for admission to Choate, having done poorly on his first try. During Jack's time at Canterbury, Rose visited only once, and Joe did not visit at all. During his time at Choate, Rose never visited the campus although Joe did.

Jack entered Choate on October 2, 1931. Less athletic, less outgoing, more cerebral, and less focused than his older brother, Jack nevertheless had to contend with Joe Jr.'s record. Despite his poor health, Jack participated in sports and was a tenacious player. However, he was only average in his academic work, something that prompted an extensive correspondence between Jack's father and the headmaster, George St. George. The headmaster was upbeat in his assessment of Jack's potentialities. St. George repeatedly maintained that Jack's challenge was one of immaturity, something that would improve with time and experience. Undoubtedly, Jack's continuing medical challenges contributed to some of the difficulties with his studies. He endured the typical childhood maladies like mumps, measles, chicken pox, and scarlet fever. In his four years at Choate, Jack was frequently confined to bed because of colds, influenza-like symptoms, fatigue, abdominal pain, and unexplained weight loss.

At Choate, Jack formed a friendship with K. Lemoyne Billings ("Lem"), and the two remained friends until Jack's assassination in 1963. Lem's family was less affluent than the Kennedys. In fact, the difference between the two boys' backgrounds was rather pronounced. The Kennedys were unaffected by the stock market crash of 1929, while Lem's family lost most of its wealth. Jack displayed sensitivity toward his friend's financial woes, even offering to give him money. In addition to the financial differences between the two friends, Jack was Roman Catholic while Lem was Protestant. However, this caused no friction in their friendship. Jack was attracted to Lem's sense of humor and what everyone called his infectious laughter. There was another difference between the two: Lem was sexually attracted to Jack. While his friend's homosexuality surprised Jack, it did not destroy their friendship.

When Jack and Lem were ready to leave Choate and go to college, Jack, contrary to his father's wishes, wanted to attend Princeton University with Lem. It may have been that Jack wanted to avoid the inevitable comparisons between himself and his older brother, something he had dealt with at Choate. Joe Jr. had gone to Harvard following his graduation from Choate and had also studied under Professor Harold Laski, a socialist and renowned teacher at the London School of Economics. Joe Jr. had even taken a trip under the direction of Laski to the Soviet Union. Jack's father wanted him to study under Laski for a year as well.

While his sons were getting an education, Joe Kennedy had become very active in politics. Endorsing Franklin D. Roosevelt for president in 1932, Joe hoped to profit from the Democratic candidate's victory in the election. Roosevelt defeated incumbent president Herbert Hoover, and the Democrats also added to their majorities in Congress. Roosevelt immediately launched his "New Deal," a decade-long effort to stimulate an economy suffering from the nation's worst economic depression. The multitude of jobs bills, labor reforms, public works projects, banking reforms, and the Social Security Act made Roosevelt a household name. Joe wanted a prize position in the new Democratic administration, and Roosevelt obliged by appointing him as the first head of the Securities and Exchange Commission (SEC), an agency that regulated the securities industry. This appointment came with more than a little irony. Joe had spent much of the 1920s engaged in stock market practices, like insider trading, that were made illegal by the New Deal reforms. Joe was going to regulate the market he had manipulated so successfully in the 1920s. Who better to reform a flawed system than one who knew it so well?

Joe resigned his position as head of the Securities and Exchange Commission after only a year of service hoping to become secretary of the treasury. When he stepped down in summer 1935, Joe took a vacation to London accompanied by Jack. Rose convinced her husband to take Kathleen ("Kick") with him as well and enroll her in a convent in France, just as Rose's father had sent her to the Netherlands to keep her away from her future husband. In this way, Rose, ever the advocate of order and discipline, would have her two most independent-minded children in Europe. However, things did not work out as planned. In October, Jack was hospitalized with a case of jaundice. More important, he had lost interest in the prospect of studying under Professor Laski, and he sailed home. Not wanting to compete with his older brother at Harvard and wanting to be reunited with old friends like Lem, Jack persuaded his father to let him attend Princeton University instead.

Jack had asked Lem to arrange for lodgings in Princeton, and his closest friend selected a bohemian apartment. The conditions of the apartment were far from ideal. Small, located on the top floor of a building without an elevator, the spartan accommodations came as a surprise to Joe Kennedy when he went to visit his son in New Jersey after his return home from England. Yet, Jack did not mind. He was happy to be among his friends. The fun-loving college freshman must have been overjoyed to be away from the possibility of study at the London School of Economics. However, London did have one advantage that Princeton, New Jersey, did not; namely, London was a vibrant urban center full of things to do. Jack found life in the small town of Princeton to be boring. He was unaccustomed to life in a small community. Adding to the woes was the Protestant ethos of Princeton University. Few Roman Catholics attended the school, and indeed the atmosphere of the university was somewhat hostile toward Catholicism. Jack's continuing poor health further complicated matters. He withdrew from Princeton and spent the spring semester recuperating in Florida and Arizona. In the fall, Jack pleased his father by enrolling at Harvard.

Jack majored in political science, with a focus on international relations and political theory. His transcript shows 11 courses in political science, with 10 Bs and 1 C. Despite the C, Jack's bookishness was evident to some. According to one of his professors, Payson S. Wild, Jack "really did have ability to think deeply and in theoretical terms." According to him, "Jack had a very thorough dose of Plato, Aristotle, Hobbes, Locke, and Rousseau. He wrote essays about these individuals. He had a thorough grounding of political theory."[6] A. Chester Hanford, his state and local government instructor, said that "much to my surprise, the grandson of Honey Fitz showed little absorption in state politics." However, Hanford said that Jack was interested in the more theoretical material in the course, such as federalism.[7] Arthur Holcombe recalls that he assigned a paper on how members of Congress reconcile local and national interests, and that Jack not only became interested in this project but also produced a "masterpiece."[8] As part of his education, Jack, like other students, was required to develop a reading list. In his choices, Jack revealed a keen interest in democratic political theory. He read Hamilton Armstrong's *"We or They": Two Worlds in Conflict*, Charles A. Beard's *The Economic Basis of Politics*, A. D. Lindsay's *The Essentials of Democracy*, and he prepared essays on these books. He also read Mussolini's *Autobiography, The*

Communist Manifesto by Marx and Engels, and Lenin's *State and Revolution.*

Yet, the Harvard experience for Jack was more than academic work alone. He was always interested in having fun, being mischievous, and doing unusual things. In the summer of 1937, for example, Jack and Lem Billings traveled from America to Europe, taking along Jack's Ford convertible. It was a chance for these two young Americans to see Europe before the outbreak of World War II two years later. Jack was interested in politics, while Lem was more focused on the architectural charms of Europe, particularly the great cathedrals. They began in the south of France and the Franco-Spanish border. Here, in the midst of the Spanish Civil War between the republican government and the fascist forces of General Francisco Franco, they were denied entry into Spain. Nevertheless, Jack managed to interview republican forces that had escaped into France. He noted their comments in a diary that he had taken to Europe to record political thoughts. Jack and Lem spent some time in Monte Carlo, enjoying the amenities of that city-state. They next visited Italy where they heard an address by Pope Pius XI before moving on to Germany, where the oppressive atmosphere of Nazism held sway over the nation. Jack and Lem were relieved when they entered Belgium and the Netherlands. Upon arriving in London, Jack fell ill suffering from hives for a few days. However, because of Joe Sr.'s influence, Jack and Lem enjoyed staying several nights in gentry houses in the countryside.

While his son was experiencing Europe, Joe Kennedy was maneuvering to secure the appointment as U.S. ambassador to Great Britain. Although Roosevelt had named him head of the Maritime Commission, Joe viewed the ambassadorship as a way to elevate himself socially and politically, for he held presidential ambitions for 1940. The idea of sending an Irish Catholic American to represent the United States was a novel idea, one that Franklin Roosevelt did not favor initially. However, by naming Joe ambassador to Great Britain, FDR concluded that he could remove a politically ambitious man from the race for the Democratic presidential nomination in 1940 while retaining an important link to powerful Irish Americans in the party. Accordingly, the appointment of Joseph Patrick Kennedy as U.S. ambassador was made official on December 9, 1937.

With his attractive family, the elder Kennedy became a popular figure in the city's social and political circles. Indeed, the ambassador became quite close with Neville Chamberlain, Britain's prime minister. Chamberlain was an advocate of appeasement, a policy of reducing tensions with Adolf Hitler's Germany. Part of this policy involved transferring territory back to Germany that it had yielded in the Treaty of Versailles. The victorious allies at the end of World War I had taken substantial German lands in Europe; had denied Austria, a German-speaking region of the former Austro-Hungarian Empire, the option of merging with Germany; had imposed heavy reparations on the Germans; had included 3,000,000 Germans in the new state of Czechoslovakia rather than in Germany; and had taken all of Germany's colonies. Chamberlain felt, and Kennedy agreed, that if they addressed these grievances peacefully rather than confrontationally, the peace of Europe could be preserved.

While the Kennedy family was enjoying its social position in London and while both Joe Jr. and Jack served on the embassy staff, Joe Sr. diminished his credibility in Washington, DC, by too openly siding with the British prime minister. President Roosevelt believed that Chamberlain's policy of appeasement would make war more likely, and thus Kennedy's pro-Chamberlain dispatches to Washington over time became less credible in the eyes of the president.

However, Joe Kennedy knew that if war came, it likely would involve the United States. Joe was determined to do everything in his power to protect his sons, Joe Jr., and Jack, from the dangers of military conflict in a second world war. Accordingly, as his position with Roosevelt became more tenuous, his relationship with Neville Chamberlain became closer. In the contest of British politics, Joe favored Chamberlain over the prime minister's foe, Winston Churchill, who was urging stronger measures be taken against Nazi Germany, which could plunge Europe into a major conflict. Churchill was thus a threat to the safety of the Kennedy sons.

The policy of appeasement found its fullest manifestation in the Munich Agreement of 1938. As mentioned previously, the Treaty of Versailles had left more than 3,000,000 Germans in the Czechoslovak state. The region most of these ethnic Germans inhabited was called the Sudetenland, a narrow band of territory along the

German-Czechoslovakian border. Hitler demanded that the Sudetenland be transferred to Germany. Such an action, however, would have weakened the military defenses of Czechoslovakia. Czech fortifications and defensive positions were located in the Sudetenland. Accordingly, a crisis developed with Hitler threatening war against Czechoslovakia, and indirectly Great Britain and France too. Both the British and French governments had made military commitments to defend the Czech border. They were thus under treaty obligations to declare war against Germany if that nation made a military move against Czechoslovakia. Churchill urged Chamberlain to be firm and uphold Britain's treaty commitment to Czechoslovakia. Military preparations escalated in both London and Paris. There was a real sense that Europe was going to war in 1938. However, Chamberlain and French prime minister Eduard Daladier were desperate to avoid a second European war. A meeting was called in Munich, with representatives of Britain, France, Germany, and Italy present. The Czechoslovakian government was not invited. The great powers of Europe allowed Hitler to seize the Sudetenland. Realizing that Czechoslovakia, without help from Britain and France, could not militarily resist the Germans, the Czech government reluctantly agreed to cede the ethnically German Sudetenland. War had been averted, at least for the time being. In Britain, Chamberlain was hailed as a hero who had brought "peace in our time" to Europe. Nonetheless, six months later Hitler violated the Munich agreement and seized the rest of Czechoslovakia. "Peace in our time" came to symbolize the emptiness of the appeasement policy. The failure of Chamberlain's policy ended Joseph P. Kennedy's own political aspirations because he had so publicly endorsed the failed policy. Nonetheless, he remained as U.S. ambassador until 1940.

WHY ENGLAND SLEPT

Jack, meanwhile, was closely following the events in Europe, and his study provided the foundation for his senior thesis, a work that shaped his outlook on leadership. Foremost among the themes he developed was the challenge totalitarian regimes such as Nazi Germany posed to democracies. Jack argued that to face this challenge, democracies must find a way to match the efficiency of dictatorial governments without sacrificing basic democratic principles in the process. Jack placed an emphasis on strong, effective leadership in a democracy as a way of matching the organizational strength of dictatorships. Differing from his father, Jack was critical of Neville Chamberlain and Chamberlain's predecessor Stanley Baldwin for the policy of appeasement.

Jack's thesis entitled "Appeasement at Munich: The Inevitable Result of the Slowness of the British Democracy to Change from a Disarmament Policy" displayed a historical and political sophistication unusual for someone his age. Sensing its possibilities as a book, Joe Kennedy called upon his friend *New York Times* columnist Arthur Krock to help Jack revise it for publication in 1940. It was Krock who suggested the more arresting title of *Why England Slept*, which was a paraphrase of Winston Churchill's 1938 book title *While England Slept*.

The thesis was not only a critique of Britain's leaders, but also a psychological study of the British peoples' failure to rearm sufficiently and confront the Nazi regime in Germany. Indeed, Jack began his discussion of Britain's failure with what he called the "psychology of the nation." According to him, "because of the inertia of human thought, nations, like individuals, change their ideas slowly," and this could be dangerous for a free people. This slowness, he said, was a weakness or potentially a fatal flaw for democracies like Britain and the United States. Jack emphasized that rapid responses were required of leaders during international crises such as that the British faced with the Nazis, and like he himself would later face as president with the Soviet Union. Political scientist James David Barber later noted the importance of Kennedy's approach. "This psychological emphasis pervades the entire book," in Barber's view, and provides an insightful "analysis of the British public." A failure to manipulate public opinion by political leaders is the "fundamental problem" in *Why England Slept*, according to Barber. To Jack, the answer for Britain's failure to rearm "was political," because leaders have the responsibility "of informing the nation of its true condition and arousing it from its slumbers." This, however, "would not happen without men to broadcast the facts and ring the alarm."[9]

Under Chamberlain and his predecessor Stanley Baldwin, the government was content to follow public opinion rather than lead and shape it. Britain's leadership maintained the view that armaments were a drain on the budget. Britain had won World War I, and the victory encouraged the feeling that change was unnecessary. The British, Jack wrote, "had not been shaken by the war, her system of government was the same, England's position in the world was regarded as assured. To be bothered as little as possible and to be allowed to go his peaceful way was all that the average Englishman asked."[10]

It would take "violent shocks" to change this outlook. Jack argued that the British desire to control military spending and Britain's commitment to the League of Nations were the chief obstacles to rearmament. There were other factors like the strength of pacifist movements and the British Labour Party's opposition to rearmament that contributed to the generally held belief that rearming would lead to war. Jack argued that a lack of innovation in democracies could be changed only with the most blunt measures. Democracies needed to innovate in order to defeat dictatorships, but this could only happen when a country's survival was at stake. "For the Englishman had to be *taught* the need for armaments," he said (emphasis in original). "Hard shocks" would provide the necessary education.[11] In this regard, Jack argued "fear" played a crucial educational role. The "hard shocks" that were to move the nation's psychology in the direction of change were based on fear, whether produced by the actions of dictators themselves, or, he hoped, by democratic leaders. Clearly, Jack felt that new norms of democratic governance were required. Yet, Britain suffered because democratic governing methods did not change. In any case, until fear was produced, Jack continued, a nation would not respond in a vigorous manner to outside threats. Fear produces a willingness to make sacrifices, which, in turn, causes the needed innovation. As he said, "it is only fear, violent fear, for one's security, such as the British experienced at Munich, that results in a nationwide demand for armaments."[12]

While leaders could use fear to move public opinion against dictatorships, Kennedy felt it was equally important that democratic leaders provide hope for the citizens of a democracy. Winston Churchill was Jack's model, for he did that during the difficult days of World War II when Britain seemed close to defeat and was suffering blistering German attacks from the air. Churchill held out hope that Britain would win, when it seemed to many, including Joe Kennedy, that Britain would lose the war. If Churchill is the hero of *Why England Slept*, then Stanley

Baldwin, Neville Chamberlain's predecessor as British prime minister, was Jack's example of how a democratic leader should not address his people. Baldwin failed to use fear, and, instead, instilled in the minds of the public the idea that opposition to Hitler would be pointless. For a time in the 1930s, Baldwin promoted international disarmament, arguing that there was no sure defense against attacks from the air. He articulated that view in a famous "bomber will always get through" radio speech that caused many Britons to feel hopelessness rather than fear. Hopelessness, in Jack's view, was the death knell for democracies that faced opposition from dictators. Citizens felt that nothing could be done, and that all was lost. Baldwin inspired hopelessness, not fear, and in doing so did little to move the psychology of the nation. Indeed, the Baldwin speech built the argument for appeasement, for if war is terrible, and nothing can be done to mitigate damage, then it must be avoided at all costs. As Jack wrote, "this feeling of hopelessness played an important part in forcing the Munich settlement," an event that historians treat as a fateful one in the development of the 20th century.[13] In the final analysis, Jack's first book is crucial in that much of what he said was replicated when he campaigned for president, and when he served as commander in chief during a time when nuclear war was a distinct possibility. Is it possible then that the young man of Harvard foreshadowed the older man who would lead his country through nuclear trauma in the early 1960s? The answer is that the language used by Jack in 1940 is remarkably similar to the speeches he gave in the late 1950s and early 1960s.

SERVICE IN WORLD WAR II

Jack graduated from Harvard in June 1940 and was accepted into the Stanford University School of Business Administration. He spent one academic year there, auditing a business course and taking courses in political science before deciding to seek admission to Yale Law School. Yet, his greatest interest lay in joining the armed services despite continuing back and stomach problems. Jack had registered for the draft in October 1940 and in summer 1941 sought admission to officer candidate school in both the army and navy, but failed the physical examination for both. At this point, Jack, as he would often do in the 1940s and 1950s, drew upon his father's considerable clout. Joe contacted Captain Alan Kirk, who had served as his naval attaché in the American embassy in London. Kirk ensured that Jack passed the medical exam, and he was commissioned as an ensign in September 1941, assigned to the Foreign Intelligence Branch of the Office of Naval Intelligence in Washington, DC.

The following January, the navy transferred Jack to the Charleston, South Carolina, Navy Yard, but like the post in Washington, Jack was saddled with a desk job when he yearned for action. He struggled with continuing back problems, but the navy finally deemed him fit for duty and sent him to the midshipman school at Northwestern University in Chicago. While training there, Jack became fascinated with the PT, or patrol-torpedo, boats. These fast 80-foot boats carried four torpedoes and four mounted machine guns. The nation's press carried numerous stories of the PT boat commanders' exploits, making the commands one of the most sought-after posts in the navy. Jack was one of more than a thousand applicants for 50 slots. His father once again intervened, and Jack landed a command. He then called upon his grandfather Honey Fitz to persuade Massachusetts senator David Walsh to use his position on the Naval Affairs Committee to get Jack an assignment in the war zone. As a result, the navy transferred Jack to the Solomon Islands in the South Pacific in January 1943. This was at a critical point in the war in the Pacific, as American forces began a long island-hopping campaign to put Japanese forces on the defensive and recapture the Philippines.

Initially, Jack saw little action, but in April the navy assigned him to *PT-109*. In late July he and his crew joined other PT boats in an effort to stop Japanese destroyers being used to transport supplies and men in New Guinea. In the early morning hours of August 2, with 14 other PT boats, Jack's *PT-109* was dispatched to confront four destroyers. Most of the PT boats were without radios, and amidst the confusion of battle on a very dark night, the Japanese destroyer *Amagiri* slammed into Kennedy's small boat, shearing it in half. Two crew members were killed outright, and another was badly burned. The survivors had to swim four hours to a nearby island with Jack towing the injured Pat "Pappy" McMahon by keeping the straps of his wounded comrade's life jacket in his mouth as he swam. On August 4, Jack moved his men

Skipper of PT-109, *South Pacific, 1943: Early on the morning of August 2, the patrol boat was cut in half by a Japanese destroyer, and Kennedy's subsequent actions to save his crew made him a war hero. (AP Photo)*

to another island while he sought help. When he encountered two natives Jack sent a message with them asking for assistance. PT boats arrived and rescued Jack and his crew, and Jack emerged as a war hero. War correspondents, who heard about the amazing survival story, eagerly interviewed the son of the former ambassador. There was even a front-page *New York Times* story about Jack's exploits with his photograph, "Kennedy's Son Is Hero in Pacific."[14]

After treatment for fatigue and severe lacerations over much of his body, Jack recovered sufficiently well to take command of another PT boat and engaged in considerable action in the fall of 1943. However, the combat took its toll, and the navy ordered him home in December. Following examinations and treatment for back pain, anemia, weight loss, and duodenitis (an inflammation of the small intestine) at the Mayo Clinic and Boston's New England Baptist Hospital, Jack was assigned to a Miami, Florida, PT base. His back pain worsened, and he opted for surgery in June 1944 at the Lahey Clinic in Boston.

Orthopedists believed he was suffering from a protruded disk, however, during the surgery they discovered that not to be true; they did remove some degenerative cartilage. The procedure did little to ease Jack's pain, indeed he continued to have muscle spasms in his lower back. As he slowly recovered, Jack spent some time in New York City where he met with famed journalist John Hersey who became intrigued by the *PT-109* story. He interviewed not only Jack, but also three members of his crew. Hersey's article, "Survival," appeared in the *New Yorker* and in a condensed version in *Reader's Digest.* As Americans read about Jack's heroism, his brother, Joe Jr., was preparing for a mission that would end in his death. Joe Jr., a naval aviator serving in England, had flown several antisubmarine patrols over the English Channel including on the successful June 6, 1944, D-Day assault on the Normandy beaches. Joe Jr. had agreed to pilot a bomber on August 12 packed with 10 tons of explosives. He and his copilot were to parachute from the plane and then activate a remote-control device to crash the plane into a German V-1 bomb launch site in Belgium. However, the plane exploded shortly after takeoff instantly killing both men.

While the entire family mourned the death of the eldest son, Joe Sr. was devastated. He admitted to a friend, "You know how much I had tied my whole life up to his and what great things I saw in the future for him."[15] His own presidential hopes dashed, the elder Kennedy had transferred that ambition to his son. He found the loss of Joe Jr. so painful that he could not bring himself to read *As We Remember Joe*, the privately printed book of reminiscences that Jack assembled in honor of his brother. Had he done so, Joe Sr. would certainly have found comfort particularly in Jack's poignant introduction that offered this remarkable tribute: "I think that if the Kennedy children amount to anything now or ever amount to anything, it will be due more to Joe's behavior and his constant example than to any other factor."[16]

NOTES

1. Rose Fitzgerald Kennedy, *Times to Remember* (Garden City, NY: Doubleday, 1974), p. 1.

2. Michael O'Brien, *John Kennedy: A Biography* (New York: Thomas Dunne Books, 2005), p. 23.

3. Rose Fitzgerald Kennedy, *Times to Remember*, p. 84.

4. Robert Dallek, *An Unfinished Life: John F. Kennedy, 1917–1963* (New York: Back Bay Books, 2003), p. 29.

5. Nigel Hamilton, *JFK: Reckless Youth* (London: Random House, 1993), p. 67.

6. Payson S. Wild, interview by Larry J. Hackman, November 25, 1968, John F. Kennedy Oral History Program, John F. Kennedy Library and Museum.

7. A. Chester Hanford Statement for the John F. Kennedy Library, 1965; Ibid.

8. Joan Meyers, ed., *John Fitzgerald Kennedy: As We Remember Him* (New York: Atheneum, 1965), p. 23.

9. James David Barber, *The Presidential Character: Predicting Performance in the White House*, 3rd ed. (Englewood Cliffs, NJ: Prentice-Hall, 1985), p. 266.

10. John F. Kennedy, *Why England Slept* (1940; repr., Westport, CT: Greenwood Press, 1981), p. 4.

11. John F. Kennedy, *Why England Slept*, pp. 5 and 4.

12. John F. Kennedy, *Why England Slept*, p. 6.

13. John F. Kennedy, *Why England Slept*, pp. 36–37.

14. "Kennedy's Son Is Hero in Pacific as Destroyer Splits His PT Boat," *New York Times*, August 20, 1943, p. 1.

15. Dallek, *An Unfinished Life*, p. 107.

16. Michael O'Brien, *Rethinking Kennedy: An Interpretive Biography* (Chicago: Ivan R. Dee, 2009), p. 55.

Chapter 3

CONGRESSMAN KENNEDY

After his discharge from active duty, Jack Kennedy was at loose ends. Although not keenly interested in law school or entering the business world, Jack was willing to experiment with journalism. His father, hoping to give his son some visibility for a run for political office, persuaded the Hearst newspapers to hire Jack to cover the spring 1945 United Nations conference in San Francisco. Though a favor for one of William Randolph Heart's friends, this was not a particularly large risk for the newspaper chain since it was employing not only the author of the acclaimed *Why England Slept*, but also a war hero. The papers took full advantage of the latter attribute of their new journalist by including, along with his stories, a photo of him in uniform and a reminder to readers of his *PT-109* exploits. Among 1,200 other journalists at the conference that established the new international organization, which featured delegates from 50 nations, Jack filed nearly 20 short dispatches in April and May for both the *Chicago Herald-American* and the *New York Journal-American*. He actually saw little promise for the new organization, given its limited powers and his conclusion that the Soviets so profoundly distrusted the West. He wrote to a war buddy sharing his pessimism about the dismal prospects for peace. "We must face the truth," Jack contended, "that the people have not been horrified by war to a sufficient extent" to avoid future conflicts. "War," he concluded, "will exist until that distant day when the conscientious objector enjoys the same reputation and prestige that the warrior does today."[1] The Hearst papers then sent Jack to England to report on the British elections. He interviewed many political figures and pundits, but failed to anticipate the Labor Party victory over Winston Churchill and the Conservative Party. After the elections, Jack traveled to Ireland and then accompanied Navy Secretary James Forrestal to the Potsdam Conference where President Harry Truman met with the new British prime minister Clement Atlee and Soviet premier Joseph Stalin to discuss plans for postwar Europe.

RUNNING FOR CONGRESS

Upon his return home, Jack gave a talk entitled "England and Germany: Victor and Vanquished" to the Hyannis Port, Massachusetts, Rotary Club. His performance was an inauspicious start for a young man being groomed for political office. Jack essentially read his speech, and to one observer of the remarkably thin, nervous young man, he seemed like "a little boy dressed up in his father's clothes."[2] Still, Joseph Kennedy intended to make Jack the surrogate for Joe Jr. In a 1957 interview, Joe explained he had told Jack that with his brother's death, it had become his "responsibility to run for Congress."[3] Jack conceded that he had given little thought to politics until his brother's death, and he acknowledged to his friends that his father was pushing him to run for office. While it is true that he came from a political family and that he had long been interested in public affairs, Jack was not eager to launch a political career. Both Mary Davis, his congressional secretary, and longtime friend George Smathers contended that Jack had little interest in politics even after winning office. "He told me," Smathers remembered, "he didn't like being a politician. He wanted to be a writer. He admired writers. Politics wasn't his bag at all." Smathers contended that Jack told him that his father made him run and that it was "agony" to campaign.[4]

James Michael Curley was the incumbent in the Eleventh Congressional District. In spring 1945, he announced his intention to take another run at a race for mayor. Curley, who had succeeded Jack's grandfather Honey Fitz Fitzgerald as mayor of Boston, decided to vacate his congressional seat because of an offer from Joe Kennedy to pay off the former mayor's considerable debts. Curley's victory in November prompted a primary election the following year to select a Democratic nominee to run for his seat in Congress. Even though Jack's family had strong ties to the district—both his father and mother were born there—he was a resident of Hyannis Port. So, to establish residency, Jack moved into the Bellevue Hotel, just down the hallway from his grandfather Honey Fitz. Though the district included commercial families and Harvard faculty members, it was largely composed of poor working-class ethnics, primarily Italians and Irish Catholics.

Jack's campaign in the primary election faced a host of challenges. He was the son of a very wealthy father running in one of the poorest districts in the state, which caused him to worry about connecting with the dock workers, factory hands, clerks, and waitresses whose votes he needed. Some of the Boston newspapers characterized Jack as nothing more than a rich carpetbagger. The *East Boston Leader*, for example, ran the following advertisement: "Congress seat for sale—No experience necessary—Applicant must live in New York or Florida—only millionaires need apply."[5] Most veteran politicians thought the young man's campaign was a quixotic effort. Those who gave him a chance to win resented him for not completing the proper apprenticeship of service in the state legislature. "Here was a kid," recalled Thomas "Tip" O'Neill—who later replaced Kennedy in the Eleventh District seat— "who had never run for anything in his life. He had done some newspaper work, but he had absolutely no political experience."[6] Jack also, at least initially, did not enjoy working the crowds, shaking hands, and making small talk. He came across as shy, even embarrassed, and struck many as too gaunt and weak to be an effective candidate. The awkward young candidate spoke too quickly with a scratchy voice, often stumbling over words.

Yet the campaign had many strengths. First, it had a genuine war hero. If district voters had forgotten about Jack's *PT-109* exploits, his standard stump speech included an account of his heroics following the sinking of his vessel. *Look* magazine published an article late in the primary campaign that included a photograph of Jack in his naval dress uniform, and his campaign staff, just before election day, mailed 100,000 copies of the *Readers Digest* condensed version of John Hersey's article on the *PT-109* episode in the *New Yorker*. Besides joining the American Legion, Jack also contributed to the establishment of the Joseph P. Kennedy Jr. Veterans of Foreign Wars post in the district.

Second, Joe and Jack assembled an enthusiastic and talented campaign staff that included professionals and passionate amateurs. Joe brought in veteran politico Joe Kane, who coined the campaign's slogan, "A New Generation Offers a Leader." Jack recruited skilled local political operatives like Billy Sutton and Dave Powers. John Galvin, the public relations director for the Dowd Advertising Agency, handled publicity. Friends like Jack's Choate roommate Lem Billings and Harvard roommate Torbert MacDonald, and navy pals like Jim Reed and Paul Fay, participated in at least part of the campaign. Ted Reardon, Joe Jr.'s Harvard roommate, also contributed, as did Ken O'Donnell, one of Bobby's Harvard classmates. Mark Dalton, law school graduate and navy veteran, who also handled the 1948 and 1950 races, was the campaign manager. This young campaign team, Tip O'Neill explained, was "superbly organized, with each area in the district having its own Kennedy-for-Congress secretary and its own committee."[7]

Third, the campaign had the Kennedy family. Brothers Bobby and 14-year-old Teddy worked diligently in the campaign, and sisters Eunice, Pat, and Jean, along with Rose, helped organize remarkably successful "house parties." These social events, as many as nine in an evening, offered refreshments and an opportunity for 25 to 75 women to meet the candidate after Rose spoke on his behalf. She later recollected that "the older women wanted to mother him and the younger ones wanted to marry him."[8] A large formal reception three days before the primary at the exclusive Hotel Commander in Cambridge was the culmination of these popular social gatherings. The Kennedy campaign sent engraved invitations to all registered Democratic women in the district. Nearly 1,500 women came to meet the Kennedy clan and most Boston newspapers carried stories about the event that was so large it caused traffic problems in Harvard Square. Archbishop Richard Cushing also helped out by introducing Jack to meetings at parochial schools and communion breakfasts. Joe Kennedy, of course, played a role, behind the scenes, and, most important, with his checkbook. As Joe Kane explained the secret to a successful political campaign, "The first is money and the second is money and the third is money." Joe provided about $300,000 for the campaign, a figure greater than the funds available to all the other primary candidates combined.[9] That war chest permitted the campaign to blanket the district with billboards, posters, and leaflets. Joe even used his connections with RKO Pictures to have a newsreel crew film Jack campaigning and several of the clips ran in district theaters.

Yet, Jack proved to be the most important asset of the campaign. He maintained a grueling schedule, making more than 400 speeches, visiting factory gates in the mornings and evenings, knocking on doors, and dropping into restaurants, barbershops, and taverns. He also developed a more relaxed speaking style with occasional flashes of humor. At one campaign event, for example, the moderator introduced the other candidates as young men "who came up the hard way." The audience laughed when the extremely wealthy Jack responded, "I seem to be the only person here tonight who didn't come up the hard way."[10] Beyond championing the concerns of returning veterans, notably their need for affordable housing, Jack's stance on issues dealt with the predictable economic concerns of the largely working-class electorate—the need to create jobs, to increase the minimum wage, and to expand Social Security benefits. "I have an obligation," he explained in an article published in *Look* magazine just before the primary vote, "as a rich man's son to people who are having a hard time of it."[11]

Jack won a remarkable 42 percent of the June primary vote in a field of 10 candidates and smashed Lester A. Brown, his Republican opponent, in the November election, winning more than 70 percent of the vote. Jack had emerged as one of the rising stars not only in Massachusetts politics, but also on the national scene. He was one of 13 "new faces" in a *Time* magazine article on the fall elections. Upon his arrival in the nation's capital, Jack appeared on NBC and CBS radio programs and at the National Press Club. His father, always seeking ways to raise Jack's visibility, worked skillfully behind the scenes with noted publicist Steve Hannagan to help Jack gain selection as one of the Junior Chamber of Commerce's 10 Outstanding Men of 1946. Jack joined such luminaries as famed World War II cartoonist Bill Mauldin, boxer Joe Louis, and Pulitzer Prize–winning historian Arthur Schlesinger Jr.

CONGRESSMAN KENNEDY

Although he arrived in the nation's capital amid much acclaim, Jack found the life of a congressman disappointing. President Truman and a Republican-dominated Congress faced a number of domestic and foreign challenges. Spiraling labor unrest, consumers struggling with inflation, housing shortages, and concerns about internal subversion filled the domestic agenda as the United States faced a rapidly developing Cold War with the Soviet Union. Yet, Jack found little about the life of a congressman appealing. He had no interest in the day-to-day operations of his congressional office or in visits with lobbyists and those seeking favors. He did not enjoy dealing with constituent concerns, leaving those largely to his staff in Washington and back in Boston. The seniority system and the complicated and cumbersome rules of the House frustrated him. He displayed slight deference to Democratic leaders like minority leader Sam Rayburn and minority whip John McCormick of his home state. Indeed, according to his friend Lem Billings, Jack had very little regard for most of his fellow congressmen whom he saw as "preoccupied . . . with their narrow political concerns."[12] Because of this jaded view, Jack had few close friends in the House; the others saw him as aloof. Family friend and future Supreme Court Justice William O. Douglas explained that time "was heavy on his hands . . . he had nothing of all-consuming interest. . . . He never seemed to get into the midstream of any tremendous political thought, or political action, or any idea of promoting this or reform that—nothing."[13]

To be sure, Jack did little to endear himself to his colleagues. Often late to meetings, given to casual dress, even on the House floor, and to four-day weekends, the young congressman struck the venerable Rayburn, who had served six years as speaker of the house prior to the huge Republican win in 1946, as a "cipher," a young man who didn't even bother to do his homework. More important, Jack's record of absenteeism was one of the worst in the chamber. One journalist recalled that Jack often fled to his office where he would aimlessly swing a golf club as he discussed issues. In part, Jack was so dismissive of his situation because of the anonymity of being a member of the House of Representatives. He wanted to accomplish great things and saw little chance of that happening as a congressman, particularly with the Republicans having a 57-vote advantage in the House.

Congressman: Newly elected representative John F. Kennedy (D-MA) on Capitol Hill, November 27, 1946. (AP Photo)

KENNEDY'S HEALTH

Jack's deteriorating physical condition also contributed to his lethargy. Jack, never in the best of health, faced a series of problems after the war. He suffered from chronic back pain, irritable bowel syndrome, prostatitus, respiratory infections, and frequent headaches. During the congressional campaign and his first months in office, he struck all who met him as thin and frail. Indeed, at the conclusion of the primary campaign an exhausted Jack Kennedy participated in the annual five-mile Bunker Hill parade in Charlestown and collapsed at the end. Aides took him to State Senator Robert Lee's home, and the senator said Jack was "yellow and blue" and he erroneously suspected that the candidate had suffered a heart attack. In 1947, Jack also faced a medical crisis on a trip to England.

Suffering from low blood pressure, nausea, and weakness, Jack could not get out of bed and was hospitalized in London. The attending physician diagnosed his illness as Addison's disease, and he did not expect the young American congressman to live a year. "In 1947, Addison's

disease," according to James N. Giglio, the historian who has most carefully examined Kennedy's medical records, "was considered to be fatal
because of the inability of the adrenal glands to produce the necessary
hormones to sustain life."[14] Treatment at the time included the implan-
tation of a pellet of a synthetic substance called desoxycorticosterone
acetate (DOCA) in the patient's thigh every few months so the body
could slowly absorb the steroid. However, the treatment could not improve life expectancy beyond about 10 years. This prospect, combined
with the death of his brother in the war and his sister Kathleen's death
in a plane crash over France in 1948, most likely caused Jack to become
a fatalist. Friends noted that Jack talked much about death over the
next couple of years and that he did not expect to live beyond the age
of 45. Thus, there is little doubt that Jack's pessimism contributed sig-
nificantly to his poor performance as a congressman.

DOMESTIC AND FOREIGN POLICY ISSUES

Still, there were a few issues that drew Jack's attention in his first term
in Congress. His assignments included the Committee on Education
and Labor and the Veterans' Affairs Committee. On the latter committee he served on a subcommittee devoted to veterans' housing, and he
used that assignment to launch into a crusade for public housing. Having walked his working-class district so thoroughly during the campaign,
Jack saw a clear need for public housing. The Depression and World
War II had slowed housing starts dramatically, forcing many couples to
move in with other families or to live in rooming houses or hotels. The
situation remained particularly acute for veterans. In Boston, for example, almost half of married veterans lived with other families. Jack
spoke not only on the House floor for a public housing bill, but also
at forums in Chicago and Boston. The Taft-Ellender-Wagner Housing
Bill would not only have appropriated funds for public housing, but
also would have maintained rent controls in federal projects. When it
failed to gain passage in 1947, Jack angrily charged that Republican
leaders were guilty of "crass ignorance" on the issue.[15]

Jack correctly perceived the Taft-Hartley Bill as an effort to undermine the gains made by organized labor under the 1935 Wagner Act. It
imposed bans on closed shops and sympathy strikes as well as enabling

the president to seek a court injunction to block a strike up to 80 days if he believed the job action would threaten the national safety or health. Jack was one of only 79 congressmen to vote against the bill and one of only 83 who voted to sustain President Truman's veto of the bill. He even debated California freshman congressman Richard Nixon in McKeesport, Pennsylvania, arguing that the proposed law would "strangle by restraint the American labor movement."[16] In the end, Republicans mustered the votes to override the veto.

Although the Congress of Industrial Organization gave him a perfect score for his voting record on labor issues, Jack was not uncritical of organized labor. Particularly troubling to him was evidence of communist influence with some union leaders. Appointed to a subcommittee to investigate communist infiltration of labor unions, he participated in hearings investigating a strike by the United Auto Workers in 1941. He closely questioned union leaders seeking to show that they acted in collusion with the USSR to inhibit U.S. war mobilization. A federal court later found that Harold Christoffel, one of the union leaders, had lied when he testified that he had not been a member of the Communist Party. During a Massachusetts stop in his 1952 presidential campaign, Adlai Stevenson reminded the crowd that "it was Congressman Kennedy and not Senator Nixon who got the first citation of a Communist for perjury."[17] Clearly concerned about the internal communist threat, Jack voted to fund the House Un-American Activities Committee as it sought to identify communists and "fellow travelers" among public employees and in the movie industry. In a survey conducted by *Cosmopolitan* magazine he agreed that eliminating subversive threats was a leading challenge for the nation. He also voted for the McCarran Internal Securities Act that compelled communist and communist-front organizations to register with the federal government. When Senator Joseph McCarthy began his quest to identify communist subversion in public life, Jack believed, "He may have something."[18] He was not alone. Most Americans, including those in his district, were hardliners on the internal communist threat. An overwhelming majority of Americans believed communists should be required to register with the Justice Department and that they should be barred from jobs in the defense industry.

At the same time, Jack demonstrated an occasional maverick spirit. In his first year in the House, Boston mayor James Michael Curley was sentenced to prison for mail fraud. When House minority whip and fellow Massachusetts congressman John McCormack asked him to join the rest of the Massachusetts delegation in a request to President Truman to commute Curley's sentence, Jack refused, obviously mindful of the differences his grandfather Honey Fitz had had with Curley. Jack also joined Republicans in their condemnation of the Truman administration over its China policy. When Communist forces under Mao Tse-Tung routed the Nationalists under Chiang Kai-shek in 1949, Jack blamed not only Truman for the "loss" of China, but also President Roosevelt for permitting the Soviets to have undue influence in the Far East, notably letting them have the Kurile Islands.

On balance, during his six lackluster years in the House, Jack remained fundamentally a New Deal Democrat who supported "bread and butter" issues important to the voters in his district—increases in the minimum wage, public housing, and unemployment insurance. Yet, there was clear evidence that, at heart, he was a fiscal conservative. He railed against deficit spending, and in a speech at Notre Dame University in 1950, Jack warned the audience about the "ever expanding power of the Federal government." He lamented the global trend of consigning "major problems into the all absorbing hands of the great Leviathan—the state."[19] In foreign affairs, despite his criticism of Truman's China and Korea policies, he supported the president's major initiatives, including the Truman Doctrine, which called for U.S. aid to Greece and Turkey to blunt Soviet advances, the Marshall Plan that promoted the economic recovery of Western European nations, and the establishment of the North Atlantic Treaty Organization, a defensive alliance to defend member nations from attack by the Soviets. Yet, as biographer Robert Dallek has pointed out, Jack "was less interested in what he could accomplish in the House, . . , than in using the office as a political launching pad."[20]

PREPARING FOR A STATEWIDE OFFICE CAMPAIGN

While the Eleventh District seat likely would have been safely his for decades, Jack had no interest in continuing in the House of Representatives, a body where he wielded little influence. As he told one aide, "I'm not going to stay in the House. I'm not challenged there."[21] Brighter prospects for his long-term health bolstered his decision to seek higher office. In 1949, researchers had developed synthetic corticosteroids (cortisone), which Jack took orally in addition to the DOCA implants, a development that promised a much longer life expectancy. Jack decided to challenge popular incumbent Republican senator Henry Cabot Lodge in the 1952 election. He had begun to lay the groundwork for a run for either the Senate or statewide office in Massachusetts in 1949. Almost every weekend that Congress was in session, Jack would fly back to Massachusetts to give speeches to veteran, fraternal, and civic groups, while maintaining an index card file on people who might be helpful in a future campaign. Over the three years, Jack spoke virtually everywhere in the Bay State. While he discussed a number of domestic issues, notably economic challenges for Massachusetts and the threats of internal subversion, Jack increasingly focused upon foreign policy issues.

In 1951, he took two foreign trips, according to his brother Ted, "to sharpen his awareness of Soviet colonial pressure in several nations."[22] The first was to Europe where he had an audience with Pope Pius XII and a meeting with Yugoslavia's premier Marshall Tito. His second trip to a number of Middle Eastern and Asian nations including Israel, Iran, India, and Japan was critical in his evolving views on America's place in the postwar world. Particularly important was his stop in Saigon. Because the French could not control the Vietminh guerrilla forces in the countryside of Indochina, Jack was unable to travel beyond the city. He talked to French officials and reporters and encountered a weak imperial nation that ruled with disdain over its colonial subjects. Overall, the lengthy fact-finding mission, according to his brother Robert who accompanied him, made a "very, very major impression" on Jack.[23] While he remained a committed cold warrior, Jack concluded that the United States must better understand the rising nationalism among Arab and Asian peoples. Rather than support colonial regimes like those of the French in Indochina, the United States would be better served in its global struggle with the Soviet Union if it supported the aspirations of noncommunist nationalist groups in Asia and the Middle East. He argued, for example, that "U.S. policymakers did not understand that Arab nationalism was the dominant force in the Middle East."[24] Upon his return, he shared his conclusions in a speech on the Mutual Broadcasting Company and in testimony before the Senate Foreign Relations and Armed Services Committees.

In his six years in Congress, Jack had not emerged as an influential figure in the House, for he had sponsored no significant legislation. Yet, he had begun to develop some independent views. He had tempered his support of issues important to his working-class constituents with a concern over the growth of the welfare state. As he became more familiar with the rising spirit of nationalism in Asia and the Middle East, Jack had begun to raise questions about the American approach to dealing with the global threat of communism, believing that the Cold War with the Soviets could not be won by neglecting the growing anticolonial sentiment. He also alienated many liberals by supporting the campaign against internal subversives. Yet, his extensive campaigning had made him a familiar face throughout Massachusetts, and he enjoyed widespread positive treatment in most of the state's newspapers. Early on, the *Worcester Sunday Telegram* had dubbed him, "the grand hope of the Democrats in this state."[25] With newer, more effective treatment available to help him deal with Addison's disease, Jack had the stamina to seek higher office. More confident about his health, more sure about his views on the major issues of the day, Jack began to assemble a campaign staff for the daunting challenge of facing Senator Henry Cabot Lodge in the 1952 election.

NOTES

1. Joan Blair and Clay Blair Jr., *The Search for JFK* (New York: Berkley Medallion Books, 1976), p. 379.

2. Michael O'Brien, *John Kennedy: A Biography* (New York: Thomas Dunne Books, 2005), p. 191.

3. Robert Dallek, *An Unfinished Life: John F. Kennedy, 1917–1963* (New York: Back Bay Books, 2003), p. 118.

4. Blair and Blair Jr., *Search for JFK*, pp. 512 and 524.

5. Dallek, *An Unfinished Life*, p. 126.

6. Tip O'Neill, with William Novak, *Man of the House: The Life and Political Memoirs of Speaker Tip O'Neill* (New York: Random House, 1987), p. 74.

7. O'Neill, *Man of the House*, p. 74.

8. Rose Fitzgerald Kennedy, *Times to Remember* (Garden City, NY: Doubleday, 1974), p. 319.

9. Michael O'Brien, *John Kennedy*, p. 196.

10. Michael O'Brien, *John Kennedy*, p. 197.

11. Michael O'Brien, *John Kennedy*, p. 200.

12. Dallek, *An Unfinished Life*, p. 137.

13. Herbert S. Parmet, *Jack: The Struggles of John F. Kennedy* (New York: Dial Press, 1980), p. 167.

14. James N. Giglio, "Growing Up Kennedy: The Role of Medical Ailments in the Life of JFK, 1920–1957," *Journal of Family History* 31 (October 2006): 375.

15. Blair and Blair Jr., *Search for JFK*, p. 541.

16. Parmet, *Jack*, p. 185.

17. Parmet, *Jack*, p. 250. The Nixon reference was to the conviction of Alger Hiss for denying that he knew communist Whitaker Chambers.

18. Dallek, *An Unfinished Life*, p. 162.

19. Parmet, *Jack*, p. 189.

20. Dallek, *An Unfinished Life*, p. 135.

21. Lawrence F. O'Brien, *No Final Victories: A Life in Politics from John F. Kennedy to Watergate* (Garden City, NY: Doubleday, 1974), p. 17.

22. Edward M. Kennedy, *True Compass: A Memoir* (New York: Twelve, 2009), p. 103.

23. Peter Collier and David Horowitz, *The Kennedys* (London: Pan Books, 1984), p. 221.

24. Michael O'Brien, *John Kennedy*, p. 235.

25. Michael O'Brien, *John Kennedy*, p. 220.

Chapter 4

SENATOR KENNEDY

Jack Kennedy preferred to run for the U.S. Senate rather than for governor of Massachusetts. He once had dismissed the state's chief executive office as one that did little more than distribute "sewer contracts." However, he had to wait until Democratic governor Paul Dever decided if he would seek a third term or would challenge the incumbent Republican Henry Cabot Lodge for a Senate seat. Dever and Kennedy met four times before the former informed the young congressman that he would seek reelection. Whether it was Dever or Kennedy, a run against Lodge clearly presented a formidable challenge. It would take a well-funded, well-organized all-out effort to unseat the incumbent. The 50-year-old Lodge was a Harvard graduate from a patrician family. A two-term senator who had resigned his seat to go on active duty in World War II, Lodge had won the 1946 contest with nearly 60 percent of the vote. Moreover, as Jack's mother Rose explained, "Lodge was tall, handsome, charming, intelligent." She frankly acknowledged that "it was difficult to imagine that Jack could win against him."[1] There were many doubts about his chances in Washington as well. Evelyn Lincoln, eventually his senate secretary, recalled that Washington insiders considered Kennedy a "lightweight" and a "playboy," and questions circulated about his health.

1952 SENATE CAMPAIGN

Jack's father once again played a significant role. Initially, he was involved in all aspects of the campaign, including the development of policy positions and speech preparation. However, as had been the case in Jack's congressional races, Joe's most important role was as a banker. He poured more than a million dollars into the effort, paying for offices, billboards, advertisements on radio and television, as well as in newspapers, and his son's campaign trips. He even loaned $500,000 to the owner of the *Boston Post,* who was facing bankruptcy, after the newspaper endorsed his son. While there is no direct evidence of a deal, Jack later told journalist Fletcher Knebel that his father had to buy the "paper or I would have lost the election."[2] Yet, Joe's constant criticism of Mark Dalton, the campaign manager, drove the man who had directed all three of Jack's successful congressional campaigns to resign.

The campaign limped along until Jack brought in his brother Bobby to be campaign manager and appointed Lawrence O'Brien to direct the organization. Although he had worked in Jack's 1946 congressional campaign, Bobby had no experience managing a campaign and he was painfully awkward speaking on his brother's behalf. His first effort was remarkably short: "My brother Jack couldn't be here. My mother couldn't be here. My sister Eunice couldn't be here. My sister Pat couldn't be here. My sister Jean couldn't be here. But if my brother Jack were here, he'd tell you Lodge has a very bad voting record. Thank you."[3] Still, he brought an extraordinary commitment to the effort, frequently putting in 18-hour days. He also had the good fortune to work with a veteran campaign director in Larry O'Brien, a former public relations man who had handled three congressional campaigns for Massachusetts congressman Foster Furcolo. O'Brien recruited more than 300 "secretaries," or local campaign directors who, in turn, recruited numerous volunteers. He gave each a manual with instructions on nuts-and-bolts matters such as voter registration. O'Brien also drove Bobby around the state to meet the secretaries. This statewide network enabled the campaign to draw upon an army of volunteers, O'Brien explained, to use telephone campaigns, mailings, tabloid distribution, registering voters, and getting them to the polls on Election Day.[4]

As in the congressional races, the Kennedy women—Rose; Jack's sisters Pat, Eunice, and Jean; and Bobby's wife Ethel—threw themselves into the campaign. They revived the successful receptions of Jack's first campaign. There were more than 30 gatherings attracting 75,000 people. Typically, Rose would make opening remarks, and Jack would then give a short stump speech and then greet those in attendance. Jack also appeared with his mother and two of his sisters on a television program called "Coffee with the Kennedys." According to one reporter, "It was an unrehearsed, homey little affair in which the Kennedys chattered on a sofa, then invited the viewers to telephone the station—collect—any questions they wanted Jack to answer during the program."[5]

However, as in 1946, the campaign's biggest asset was Jack. With the nation still at war in Korea and deeply engaged in a Cold War with the Soviet Union, the campaign staff continued to exploit his heroics in World War II, distributing nearly a million copies of an account of the *PT-109* episode. More important, Jack had become a seasoned campaigner. Compared to his first run for Congress in 1946, he was more comfortable speaking either to large crowds or to small groups. He was also at ease on television. For example, in December 1951, before the campaign even began, Jack appeared on NBC's *Meet the Press* and ably fielded questions on corruption in the Truman administration, the Soviet threat in Western Europe, the potential Democratic presidential nominee for the 1952 election, and on what he had learned on his extensive trip to the Middle East and Far East. When asked if he would be a candidate for the U.S. Senate, Jack quickly responded, "I'd like to go to the Senate." "I'm seriously considering running." He was particularly effective with individual voters. "He had the ability," Larry O'Brien recalled, "to focus exclusively on each person for a few seconds, establishing real human contact, making the person feel that he would remember and treasure those few seconds of conversation."[6]

His success in projecting the image of a refined and congenial candidate, along with the solid organization of his staff, served Jack well in a campaign where personality trumped issues. Because both men "in a relative sense, are progressive," and supported President Truman's fundamental foreign policy ventures, a *New York Times* article concluded, "the issues in this campaign are something less than explosive."[7] For many, the race pitted an incumbent who represented Protestant Anglo-Saxons against a challenger who became the standard bearer for Catholic immigrants, despite Jack's "lace curtain" Irish Catholic upbringing. While Jack succeeded in making voters from all groups comfortable with him in personal appearances, the urbane Lodge seemed distant. Moreover, Lodge started his campaign late and did poorly in debates with his young rival. Because he had helped persuade Dwight Eisenhower to run for the presidency and had served as the general's preconvention campaign manager, Lodge not only lost valuable time for his own campaign, but also alienated the Massachusetts supporters of conservative Ohio senator Robert A. Taft who had sought the presidential nomination. While Dever lost the governor's race to Republican Christian Herter and Eisenhower easily defeated Adlai Stevenson in Massachusetts, Jack defeated Lodge by 70,000 votes. It had been a remarkable campaign. Two journalists who later wrote about the 1952 senate race called the Kennedy effort "the most methodical, the most scientific, the most thoroughly detailed, the most intricate, the most disciplined and smoothly working state-wide campaign in Massachusetts history—and possibly anywhere else."[8]

SENATOR JOHN KENNEDY

Because of his dramatic victory over a popular incumbent senator in a year when Dwight Eisenhower defeated the top of the ticket, Jack took office with celebrity status and managed to retain it throughout the 1950s. He appeared on television programs like *Meet the Press, Person to Person, Face the Nation,* and *Omnibus.* In 1953, for example, his appearance on *Person to Person,* the popular Edward R. Murrow interview program, gave Jack the opportunity to discuss his *PT-109* exploits, his advocacy of improved strategic air power, his views on the Taft-Hartley Act, and the need to boost Social Security payments and the minimum wage. He eagerly embraced the media, responding to countless requests for interviews, and his cooperation with the journalists led to many articles in major newspapers such as the *New York Times.* He also appeared on the cover of *Life* magazine three times and on *Time's* cover twice. There were also articles in *Look*, *American Mercury*, and the *Saturday Evening Post*. The latter magazine in 1957 characterized Jack as "trustworthy, loyal, brave, clean and reverent, boldly facing up to the challenges of the Atomic Age." A *Time* cover story the same year declared, "Jack Kennedy has left panting politicians and swooning women across a large spread of the U.S."[9]

Jack's stunning win energized the young senator. As he began his tenure in the Senate, those around him were struck by his enthusiasm, excitement, and engagement in the business of the upper chamber. Nevertheless, Jack saw many senators who fit the mold of the congressmen he had criticized in 1947. Too many senators, he believed, were "cautious, self-serving, and unheroic, more often than not the captive of one special interest or another."[10] Yet, Jack was in a bigger, more influential arena of power and quickly set about making his mark. As he had done as a congressman, Jack left the mundane affairs of his office, such as responding to constituent concerns, to his staff, headed by Ted Reardon. There were some new faces including secretary Evelyn Lincoln, but the most important addition was Theodore Sorensen, who brought glittering credentials. He had been Phi Beta Kappa and editor of the *Law Review* at the University of Nebraska. His mother had been a suffragette, and his father had been a strong supporter of agrarian progressive Republican senator George Norris. The liberal Sorensen was both a pacifist and civil rights activist who initially worried that Jack was too soft on Joseph McCarthy. Over time, however, he became Jack's alter ego, councilor, and speechwriter. Sorensen researched legislative proposals, and more important, he wrote many speeches and articles for Jack. As he later explained, Jack did not dictate ideas for speeches, Sorensen simply wrote them knowing what his boss wanted to say. His articles in *Life*, the *New York Times Magazine*, *New Republic*, *Atlantic Monthly*, and *Vogue* with Jack's byline brought Sorensen half the royalties and fees.

Jack did not produce a significant domestic policy record during his Senate years. His efforts to revive the lackluster New England economy were unsuccessful; indeed he supported the development of the St. Lawrence Seaway, which many in the region believed would hurt Massachusetts ports. To the distress of liberals, he did not emerge as a champion of civil rights. In 1957, he refused to support an effort to place a civil rights bill on the Senate calendar, instead of sending it to the Judiciary Committee headed by segregationist James Eastland from Mississippi. He also supported a provision for jury trials for those who violated a citizen's right to vote. Civil rights supporters condemned it because they believed no Southern jury would vote to convict violators. His stance on these provisions reflected his efforts to gain the support of Southern Democrats, or, as Ted Sorensen put it more bluntly, Jack's approach to civil rights issues was "shaped primarily by political expediency instead of basic human principles."[11]

In 1957, Jack did become deeply involved in labor issues. He joined the Senate Select Committee on Improper Activities in the Labor or Management Field chaired by Arkansas Democrat John McClellan, more popularly known as the McClellan Committee, or the Rackets Committee. His brother Bobby, with a staff of 65 investigators, served as chief counsel. The committee focused its attention on the powerful Teamsters Union and its leaders Dave Beck and Jimmy Hoffa. This was a risk for Jack because organized labor leaders had come to see him as a friend because he had opposed the Taft-Hartley Act and had supported increases in the minimum wage. His father believed that a high-profile investigation would hurt Jack's chances with organized labor in a presidential run in 1960. Yet, the often-televised hearings over two years revealed a zealous Bobby Kennedy uncovering corruption and mismanagement, leading to the conviction of Beck for stealing from the union treasury and leaving an indelible image of Hoffa as a ruthless boss likely linked with organized crime. Indeed, Bobby called several mobsters like Sam Giancana, Santo Trafficante, and Carlos Marcello before the committee. Jack missed many of the hearings because of his numerous campaign trips, but sought to be present during the televised hearings. He developed a special disdain for Hoffa, noting once, "I have never met a worse man. I look across at this fellow at the hearings, and reconstruct the motives for what he is doing, and they are evil."[12]

As chair of the Senate's labor subcommittee, Jack drew upon the hearings to draft a reform labor bill imposing restrictions on union expenditures, including required audits of unions, and prohibitions against embezzlements of union funds or loans of union funds for illicit purposes. Although the bill failed to gain passage, Jack emerged in the nation's press as a courageous reformer, willing to take on corrupt union leaders. The *Saturday Evening Post,* for example, featured him and his brother in a series of articles in 1959 entitled "The Struggle to Get Hoffa."

Foreign policy questions always captured more of Jack's attention. His personal background in international affairs was substantial. He had traveled extensively in Europe twice before the war, written a best-seller on the dangers of appeasement, and had experienced the frightful dangers of war in the South Pacific. As a budding journalist, Jack had covered the founding of the United Nations, the postwar elections in England, and the Potsdam Conference. He had read widely on foreign policy matters from his undergraduate days, and he had met with political, diplomatic, and military leaders in Europe, the Middle East, and Asia on his two trips in 1951. Jack was most engaged when Senate debates focused on foreign affairs. By the mid-1950s, Jack had become a critic of President Eisenhower's "New Look" foreign policy. Concerned that large increases in defense spending would keep him from balancing the federal budget and providing tax cuts, Eisenhower had opted for a foreign policy that relied upon military assistance to friendly nations and building a substantial nuclear arsenal, rather than a large standing army. This would, according to Defense Secretary Charles Wilson, give the United States "more bang for the buck." A willingness to "go to the brink" of war with nuclear weapons, according to Secretary of State John Foster Dulles, would more effectively contain Soviet expansion than a large U.S. army.

Jack argued that the U.S. should increase military spending and adopt a more flexible foreign policy. The Eisenhower approach could not, in his judgment, effectively deal with guerilla conflicts or independence movements. To be sure, he continued to believe in a monolithic view of communism and in the validity of the domino theory, that is, if one noncommunist country fell, neighboring noncommunist nations would likely do so as well. Still, Jack argued that the Eisenhower administration had paid too little attention to the rapidly growing anticolonial sentiment in Asia, the Middle East, and Africa. In 1954, as the French faced an ever more hopeless situation in Indochina, Jack called for Vietnamese independence, not further U.S. aid, as the only viable option to the growing popularity of the communist movement there.

In an April Senate address, Jack argued that "no amount of American military assistance in Indochina can conquer an enemy that is everywhere and at the same time nowhere."[13] He repeated those sentiments on a CBS television program two days after the French garrison fell at Dien Bein Phu on May 7. Three years later, Jack denounced France again for suppressing the anticolonial movement in Algeria. In a Senate speech, he argued that the United States must stand with those peoples seeking self-determination because "the most powerful single force in the world today is neither communism nor capitalism, neither the H-bomb nor the guided missile—it is man's eternal desire to be free and independent."[14]

In 1957, Jack secured an appointment to the powerful Senate Foreign Relations Committee, and he published an article in the influential journal *Foreign Affairs*. The former gave him greater visibility and the latter gave him a rare opportunity to share his thoughts on the need for the United States to support nationalistic movements around the globe and extend more economic assistance to combat communism. Jack joined other Democratic critics of President Eisenhower in 1957 and 1958, charging that the Soviets had eclipsed the United States in the development of nuclear power plants, jet engines, and intercontinental ballistic missiles. In a Senate speech in 1958, for example, Jack claimed that Pentagon experts had predicted that between 1960 and 1964 American "missile development" would "lag so far behind the Russians as to cause a grave threat to our national existence."[15] By the end of the decade Jack had developed a coherent view of the world, one requiring a substantial U.S. investment to ensure victory in the global challenge posed by the Soviet Union.

KENNEDY AND JOSEPH McCARTHY

One of Jack's biggest challenges in the Senate was his relationship with Wisconsin senator Joseph McCarthy. From early 1950 through 1954, McCarthy became synonymous with the crusade to stop internal subversion. The Soviet development of the atomic bomb, the American "loss" of China to the communist forces under Mao Tse-Tung, and the frustrating stalemated conflict in Korea prompted some Americans in the late 1940s and early 1950s to believe that an internal conspiracy of

communists and "fellow travelers" was aiding the international communist cause and undermining the United States. An active House
Un-American Activities Committee investigated Hollywood and vigorously pursued Alger Hiss who was a high-ranking employee of the
State Department. President Truman launched a four-year loyalty investigation of federal employees, and the Congress passed the McCarran
Internal Security Act, which required all communist organizations to
register with the federal government. McCarthy began his crusade on
February 9, 1950, in a speech in Wheeling, West Virginia, where he
charged that he had a list of more than 200 communists who worked for
the State Department. A master at outrageous charges, McCarthy was
relentless despite a Senate committee's conclusion later that summer
that his charges were a "hoax and a fraud." In 1953, McCarthy became
chair of the Permanent Investigating Subcommittee of the Government Operations Committee and expanded his search for communists,
one that eventually led him to make charges against officers in the U.S.
Army. He skillfully exploited media coverage while appearing on the
covers of both *Newsweek* and *Time* magazines. His reckless approach,
one that led him to charge that General George C. Marshall was a
traitor, that Secretary of State Dean Acheson was the "Red Dean," and
that President Truman was an alcoholic "son of a bitch," eventually led
to a censure vote in the Senate.[16]

Jack had met McCarthy in the Solomon Islands during World War II.
Joe later claimed that Jack took him on rides aboard *PT 109* and
even permitted him to fire the vessel's machine guns. While Jack
claimed not to recall any of that, the Kennedy family did have close
ties to McCarthy. When he moved to Washington, McCarthy stayed
occasionally at Jack's Georgetown residence and Jack occasionally
dropped by Joe's house for backyard barbecues. McCarthy also visited
the Kennedys in Palm Beach, Florida, and on Cape Cod. He dated
Jack's sisters Pat and Jean who remembered that he would talk about
communism for a while and then "kissed very hard."[17] Joe Kennedy,
who admired McCarthy's crusade against communism, became a big
supporter of the Wisconsin senator. In 1953, Bobby worked on the
senator's committee for five months. When asked a decade later why
he had been willing to serve with McCarthy, Bobby explained, "Well,
at the time, I thought there was a serious internal security threat to

the United States, . . . and Joe McCarthy seemed to be the only one who was doing anything about it."[18]

While not as strident as McCarthy, Jack shared his concerns about communist subversion in America. He had joined McCarthy and other anticommunist political figures in criticizing Owen Lattimore. A professor at Johns Hopkins University's Walter Hines Page School of International Relations, Lattimore was a specialist in East Asian politics and development. He was active in an organization known as the Institute of Pacific Relations, editing its journal *Pacific Affairs*, and was an advisor to Chiang Kai-shek in World War II. Increasingly disillusioned with Chiang's rule, Lattimore argued that he could not win the struggle against communist forces in China and contended that further U.S. support for Chiang's regime would be unwise. In 1949, Jack argued that men like Lattimore had sadly influenced U.S. foreign policy. They had been "so concerned . . . with the imperfections of the democratic system in China after twenty years of war, and the tales of corruption in high places, that they had lost sight of our tremendous stake in a noncommunist China."[19] A year later, McCarthy named Lattimore as the "top Russian espionage agent" in the nation.[20] Jack was also delighted when Richard Nixon defeated Helen Gahagan Douglas in the California Senate race. Nixon, who called Douglas the "Pink Lady," successfully labeled the liberal Democrat as a fellow traveler who had fought the exposure of communist subversives.

Jack, always aware of political realities, also understood that the anticommunist message had particularly strong support among Irish Catholic voters in Massachusetts. On occasion Jack defended McCarthy. In February 1952, for example, at a dinner event at Harvard, a speaker noted that the university had produced neither an Alger Hiss nor a Joseph McCarthy. "How dare you," Jack responded, "couple the name of a great American patriot with that of a traitor!"[21] Jack, like most of his fellow senators, eventually concluded that McCarthy's excesses, his outlandish charges and casual acquaintance with the facts, could not be tolerated. Still, he did not join the majority of senators in censuring McCarthy. He was recovering from back surgery on December 2, 1954, when senators voted on a censure resolution, but could have utilized an obscure Senate rule to record his position on the disciplinary action. Jack could have instructed a staff member to register an "announcement" or "pair" supporting censure, but chose not to do so. He later explained, "I was caught in a bad situation. My brother was working for Joe. I was against it, I didn't want him to work for Joe, but he wanted to. And how the hell could I get up there and denounce Joe McCarthy when my own brother was working for him? So it wasn't so much a thing of political liability as it was a personal problem."[22] Theodore Sorensen, his legislative assistant, who could have registered Jack's support for the censure vote, later criticized Kennedy for his inaction, "I was—and remain—disappointed by his inaction, even though I recognize the political and personal realities behind it."[23]

KENNEDY AND *PROFILES IN COURAGE*

Jack's failure to join in the public denunciation of McCarthy prompted many liberal Democrats to question the senator's integrity, particularly in light of the publication of his *Profiles in Courage*. In 1954, Jack read Herbert Agar's biography of John Quincy Adams entitled *The Price of Union*. In it, he discovered a courageous senator who defied his party on key votes, notably in support of President Thomas Jefferson's 1807 embargo on trade with England, which threatened the economy of New England seaports. Jack admired Adams's principled stance, and his friend Charles Bartlett believed that Jack's difficulty in taking a clear public stand against McCarthy caused him to investigate how past senators had met the challenge of balancing their individual judgment against the wishes of their constituents. Whatever the case, Jack asked Ted Sorensen to research other examples of senatorial courage for a possible magazine article. Beginning in December 1954, Sorensen shipped books and other research material to Jack in Palm Beach, where he convalesced from his back surgery until May 1955. Jack focused most of his time in early 1955 on the project, reading, taking notes, and dictating his thoughts. Besides securing a contract with Harper and Row for a book, Sorensen called upon several individuals for help with the project. Jim Landis, a Kennedy family lawyer and former dean of the law school at Harvard, submitted suggestions in early May 1955. Sorensen also solicited several scholars, including James MacGregor Burns, Arthur Schlesinger Jr., and Allan Nevins, for their assistance. Most important, he called upon history professor Jules

Davids to critique the initial draft of the project. Davids, who was one of his wife Jackie's professors, offered such a helpful assessment that Jack and Sorensen prevailed upon him to write drafts of five of the book's chapters. Sorensen drafted most of the remaining chapters while Jack reviewed all the drafts and made revisions. The study of eight senators—John Quincy Adams, Daniel Webster, Thomas Hart Benton, Sam Houston, Edmund Ross, Lucius Q. C. Lamar, George W. Norris, and Robert Taft—represented Jack's attempt to explain the essence of political courage. These were men, he wrote in the opening chapter, "whose abiding loyalty to their nation triumphed over all personal and political considerations, men who showed the real meaning of courage and a real faith in democracy."[24]

Profiles in Courage, a book Theodore Sorensen called a "collaboration" and Kennedy biographer Robert Dallek considered "more the work of a 'committee' than of any one person," enjoyed immediate success upon its publication in January 1956.[25] Major newspapers like the *New York Times, Chicago Daily Tribune, Christian Science Monitor,* and *Los Angeles Times* gave it positive reviews. Jack spoke at both the National Book Awards dinner in New York City and the *Washington Post* Book and Author luncheon in February 1956. A bestseller for several months, the book sold more than 120,000 copies in its first two years. Most impressive, however, the Pulitzer Prize Committee selected *Profiles in Courage* as the best biography of 1956. There was some controversy, however, over the committee's decision. The "jurors" for the award were historians Bernard Mayo and Julian Boyd. They had recommended other biographies ahead of Jack's, but the committee ignored them. As John Hohenberg, who administered the awards explained, "at that particular point, Kennedy was so much in the news, and his book was so much admired by the editors around the table, most of whom had read it, that they overruled the biography jury."[26] Despite the success, rumors emerged that Jack had not written the book. Most prominent was columnist Drew Pearson's charge on Mike Wallace's ABC program in December 1957 that the book "was ghostwritten for him." An angry Jack retained the services of prominent Washington attorney Clark Clifford. After explaining to the senator's even more outraged father that suing ABC for $50 million was not a good idea, Clifford persuaded ABC and Pearson to issue retractions after showing them sample chapters, Jack's research notes, and testimony from the book's editor Evan Thomas and *New York Times* columnist Arthur Krock who both said they observed Jack working on the manuscript.

JACQUELINE KENNEDY AND OTHER WOMEN

In 1951, Jack met Jacqueline Bouvier, the stepdaughter of wealthy lawyer and stockbroker Hugh D. Auchincloss. She had studied at Vassar and the Sorbonne before graduating at George Washington University. An elegant woman fluent in several languages, with an interest in art, opera, and ballet and from a prominent family, Jackie seemed a perfect mate for the politically ambitious Kennedy. They courted for two years, but delayed announcing their engagement until the *Saturday Evening Post* published a feature article on Jack entitled "The Senate's Gay Young Bachelor." Married in September 1953, they were a most photogenic couple and were a hit on Edward R. Murrow's *Person to Person* television program on CBS a month later. However, Jack's frequent absences from home on campaigns and Senate work, along with his refusal to stop his womanizing, created problems for their marriage. One of the low points, an episode that demonstrated his indifference, occurred shortly after the Democratic Convention in 1956. Jack went sailing off the French coast with longtime friend George Smathers while Jackie was in her seventh month of pregnancy. When she had a stillborn girl, the family had trouble reaching Jack, and when he heard the news, Smathers had to persuade him to return home to preserve his marriage.

From his days at Choate, through his adult life, Jack was sexually promiscuous. During World War II he had an affair with Inga Arvad, whom the FBI had under surveillance believing that she was a Nazi spy. After the war he vigorously pursued attractive women, often for casual, usually one-night affairs, but also in a few other cases, for long-term relationships. Some were secretaries and flight attendants; others were prominent, accomplished women, such as model and fashion editor Florence "Flo" Pritchett, English tennis star Kay Stammers, and actress Gene Tierney, who once sat in the congressional balcony to watch him debate. But there were also strippers Blaze Starr and Tempest Storm. Sometimes he met women in New York at swank nightclubs or had

Jack Kennedy marries Jacqueline Bouvier at her stepfather's estate in Newport, RI, September 12, 1953. (AP Photo/Cecil Yates)

a rendezvous at the Carroll Arms Hotel just across the street from his Senate office. He even had his secretary Evelyn Lincoln arrange dates for him. Fellow congressman Tip O'Neill recalled, "He had more fancy young girls flying in from all over the country than anyone could count," and longtime associate Ted Sorensen noted that while campaigning Kennedy "was unfailingly flirtatious with all young women, particularly pretty, single women."[27]

There have been several attempts to explain Jack's behavior: that he was emulating the behavior of his father; that he believed it was a perquisite of the privileged class; that he was a fatalist believing he had such a short time to live; that he was seeking a sense of self; or that he sought to relieve the stresses of his job. Whatever the correct explanation, his philandering continued after his marriage, through his presidency. The long list of women included prostitute and suspected East German spy Ellen Rometsch; Judith Campbell, who was also having an affair with organized crime leader Sam Giancana; and film star

Marilyn Monroe, with whom he had a brief liaison. Jack's view on fidelity in marriage, beyond the unmistakable evidence of his affairs, was captured in a conversation with his brother Ted on the latter's wedding day in 1958. He reminded his younger sibling "being married didn't really mean that you had to be faithful to your wife."[28]

CONTINUING HEALTH PROBLEMS

Jack suffered a series of maladies during the 1950s. Addison's disease remained a threat especially when he neglected to take his medications, as was the case during his trip to Asia in 1951. On Okinawa, his temperature rose to 106, and the physicians treating him thought he would die. His back pain was constant, in part due to his actions. He loved playing touch football, and during the 1952 Senate campaign, while at a Springfield, Massachusetts, fire station, he decided to slide down the fire pole. When he landed he was in agony. For weeks afterward, he had to use crutches, and each night he had to soak in hot water before retiring. The back pain only got worse. Treatment at George Washington University Hospital in 1953 failed to help. By early 1954, Jack was dependent on crutches, unable to pick up things from the floor and in so much pain that he often remained in the Senate chamber after quorum calls, dictating to his secretary from the back row of the chamber. Finally, he decided upon back surgery, even though the risks were enormous. Most Addison's patients did not survive major surgery because of their greater susceptibility to life-threatening infections. Indeed, his physicians warned him that his chance of surviving the surgery were only 50-50. In October 1954, surgeons in New York performed a "lumbo-sacral fusion together with a sacroiliac fusion." Simply put, the surgeons used a metal plate and a bone graft to stabilize his spine. Predictably, he suffered both a urinary tract infection and a staphylococcal infection. After he slipped into a coma, a priest administered the last rites. He recovered sufficiently to leave the hospital in December for recuperation at the Kennedy vacation home in Palm Beach, only to return to New York to have surgeons remove the metal plate used in the fusion of the lower spine because it had caused a staph infection. The surgery did not eliminate all the pain. Jack ultimately came to rely upon Dr. Janet Travell's injections of procaine and Novocain for relief.

U.S. senator: John F. Kennedy (D-MA), with his wife, Jacqueline, returns to the Senate in May 1955 after a long convalescence from spinal surgery in October 1954 and February 1955. (AP Photo)

Travell also recommended a lift in his left shoe for his shortened left leg and persuaded him that sitting in a rocking chair would also help relieve the pain. In all, Jack faced nine hospitalizations between 1953 and 1957, because of back pain, urinary tract infections, prostatitus, diarrhea, and dehydration.

PREPARING FOR A WHITE HOUSE RUN

Joseph Kennedy initially believed that the best way to position his son for a presidential run was to have him run as a vice presidential candidate in 1956. To that end, believing that Adlai Stevenson had no chance to defeat Dwight Eisenhower, he offered to finance Senate Majority Leader Lyndon Johnson's campaign if he agreed to take Jack as his running mate. When Johnson refused, the senior Kennedy concluded that his son should not pursue the vice presidential nomination if Stevenson headed the ticket, believing that Jack would be partially blamed for the loss. However, Jack decided it worth a run as did some journalists. Fletcher Knebel, in feature articles in *Look* magazine in February and June of 1956, argued that Jack's youth, military background, and past electoral success made him an attractive candidate, and he further argued that Jack's Catholic faith posed no barrier. The always dependable Ted Sorensen produced a detailed study of nearly two dozen potential running mates showing Jack as the pick of the lot. Both Sargent Shriver, Eunice Kennedy's husband, and Ted Sorensen personally lobbied Stevenson to name Jack his running mate. Yet, Stevenson could not be convinced, believing that he needed a Southern candidate.

Still, the Democratic Convention in Chicago provided Jack several opportunities for positive national exposure. Because of the success of *Profiles in Courage*, Hollywood producer Dore Schary selected Jack to narrate a documentary film screened on the first night of the convention. Stevenson then asked Jack to make the presidential nominating speech, which the young senator believed was a goodwill gesture by Stevenson for not picking him as a running mate. Instead, Stevenson selected no one, throwing the nomination open to the convention. Jack's staff mustered a remarkable effort, but after leading on the second ballot, Jack lost to Estes Kefauver, the liberal senator from Tennessee. Once the balloting had ended, Jack made a gracious concession speech and called for Kefauver's nomination by acclamation. The five days in Chicago made Jack a national political celebrity. Newspapers lauded him as a charismatic, vigorous, articulate, and gracious competitor. Stevenson wrote to a friend, "I have a feeling that he was the real hero of the hour and that we shall hear a great deal more from this promising young man."[29]

Jack campaigned hard for Stevenson and Kefauver, appearing all across the country logging more than 30,000 miles. He delivered more than 150 speeches calling for more social programs to help workers, farmers, and small business men while advocating a new foreign policy that would align the United States more with the impulse for self-determination in Asia and Africa and less with European imperial powers. Even though the Stevenson campaign floundered, Jack was a big draw. In San Francisco, for example, the local press labeled him as the "fast rising star" of the Democratic Party. "The grinning Kennedy," the *San Francisco Examiner* noted in its coverage of his speech at the Fairmont Hotel, "his boyish charm belying his noted political aggressiveness, got a standing ovation when he entered the hotel's Gold Room, another when he was introduced . . . and still another when he finished speaking."[30] Jack also appeared on a segment of *Meet the Press* and in a campaign film with Stevenson. His travel was part of what became a four-year campaign for the presidential nomination in 1960. Traveling most of the time with just Ted Sorensen, Jack visited every state. Sorensen maintained an extensive file of supporters and influential people in each state, and Jack also made campaign contributions to key supporters who were running for office. In the midst of this extraordinary national effort, he ran a remarkably successful reelection campaign in Massachusetts in 1958. His staff, headed by Larry O'Brien and Kenneth O'Donnell, blitzed the state with more than a million pieces of campaign literature, gained more than 300,000 signed pledges of support, dispatched an army of volunteers knocking on doors, and sent the senator to communities all across the state. The result was a victory with the largest majority—he won nearly 74 percent of the votes—of any candidate for the Senate that year.

As the campaign for the White House began in 1960, Jack had prepared well. He had sponsored no major legislation and had held no significant positions in either the House or the Senate. Yet, he had skillfully covered up his numerous health problems. Indeed, when asked point blank about Addison's disease, he consistently denied it. In 1959, for example, he told Arthur Schlesinger Jr., "No one who has Addison's disease ought to run for President; but I do not have it and have never had it."[31] More important, Jack had established a well-deserved reputation as a diligent campaigner and winner. Tip O'Neill recognized this early in the 1950s, calling Jack "the hardest-working candidate that I ever saw in my life."[32] He had also gained recognition as a vibrant new voice in national politics particularly on foreign policy questions due largely to what James Giglio, one of his biographers, has called "manufactured imagery." "Getting much attention," Giglio explained, "was the war hero, the Pulitzer Prize-winning intellectual, and the youthful, robust leader who vowed—in the wake of the somnolent Eisenhower era—to get America 'moving again'."[33]

NOTES

1. Rose Fitzgerald Kennedy, *Times to Remember* (Garden City, NY: Doubleday, 1974), p. 319.

2. Michael O'Brien, *John Kennedy: A Biography* (New York: Thomas Dunne Books, 2005), p. 257.

3. Peter Collier and David Horowitz, *The Kennedys* (London: Pan Books, 1984), p. 221.

4. Lawrence F. O'Brien, *No Final Victories: A Life in Politics from John F. Kennedy to Watergate* (Garden City, NY: Doubleday, 1974), p. 35.

5. Michael O'Brien, *John Kennedy*, p. 250.

6. Lawrence F. O'Brien, *No Final Victories*, p. 33.

7. Cabell Phillips, "Case History of a Senate Race," *New York Times Sunday Magazine*, October 26, 1952, p. 50.

8. Robert Dallek, *An Unfinished Life: John F. Kennedy, 1917–1963* (New York: Back Bay Books, 2003), p. 173.

9. Michael O'Brien, *John Kennedy*, p. 328.

10. Dallek, *An Unfinished Life*, p. 177.

11. Herbert S. Parmet, *Jack: The Struggles of John F. Kennedy* (New York: Dial Press, 1980), p. 409.

12. Michael O'Brien, *John Kennedy*, p. 380.

13. Collier and Horowitz, *The Kennedys*, p. 246.

14. Dallek, *An Unfinished Life*, p. 222.

15. "Kennedy Urges Arms Cut Drive," *New York Times*, August 15, 1958, p. 2.

16. David Oshinsky, "In the Heart of Conspiracy," *New York Times*, January 27, 2008, http://www.nytimes.com/2008/01/27/review/Oshinsky-t.html (accessed March 22, 2010).

17. Evan Thomas, *Robert Kennedy: His Life* (New York: Simon & Schuster, 2002), p. 65.

18. Thomas, *Robert Kennedy*, p. 64.

19. Dallek, *An Unfinished Life*, p. 160.

20. Donald F. Crosby, *God, Church, and Flag: Senator Joseph R. McCarthy and the Catholic Church, 1950–1957* (Chapel Hill: University of North Carolina Press, 1978), p. 57.

21. Dallek, *An Unfinished Life*, p. 162.

22. Dallek, *An Unfinished Life*, p. 191.

23. Theodore C. Sorensen, *Counselor: A Life at the Edge of History* (New York: HarperCollins, 2008), p. 155.

24. John F. Kennedy, *Profiles in Courage* (1956; reissue, New York: HarperCollins, 2003), p. 18.

25. Dallek, *An Unfinished Life*, p. 199.

26. Parmet, *Jack*, pp. 396–397.

27. Tip O'Neill, with William Novak, *Man of the House: The Life and Political Memoirs of Speaker Tip O'Neill* (New York: Random House, 1987), p. 87 and Sorensen, *Counselor*, p. 116.

28. Dallek, *An Unfinished Life*, p. 195.

29. Michael O'Brien, *John Kennedy*, p. 322.

30. Michael O'Brien, *John Kennedy*, p. 324.

31. Arthur Schlesinger Jr., *Journals, 1952–2000* (New York: Penguin Press, 2007), p. 58.

32. Michael O'Brien, *John Kennedy*, p. 248.

33. James N. Giglio, *The Presidency of John F. Kennedy*, 2nd ed. (Lawrence: University Press of Kansas, 2006), p. 16.

Chapter 5

THE 1960
PRESIDENTIAL CAMPAIGN

The 1960 presidential campaign had its origins in a Soviet technological breakthrough in the 1950s. On October 4, 1957, the Soviet Union launched the world's first satellite, *Sputnik*. The Soviet demonstration of its advanced technology in orbit stunned the American public. A national debate emerged over the failure of American science to compete with that of the Soviet Union. Americans wanted to know why their nation had apparently failed in this crucial area. Clearly, many thought, it demonstrated Soviet superiority in rocketry. This was no simple fear of losing prestige. It was, instead, a fear among many Americans that their survival was at stake. Unless the United States improved its scientific and technological standing, then the Soviets might overtake the United States in military superiority. Articles in newspapers and magazines all presented *Sputnik* as a failure of the United States scientifically, and urged a vigorous response. *Sputnik* was a godsend for John F. Kennedy. It contributed to the conditions that led to his successful run for president in 1960.

Although Jack did not receive the vice presidential nomination in 1956, it certainly enhanced his standing for the 1960 Democratic presidential nomination. There was no shortage of prominent Democrats seeking the nomination. Missouri's Democratic senator Stuart Symington, who had the support of former president Harry S. Truman, was regarded as everyone's second choice for the nomination. Hubert Humphrey, the ambitious, liberal senator from Minnesota, was unpopular in the South, but would be a formidable opponent for Jack in Northern primaries. Humphrey had strong backing from labor unions who were a critical part of the Democratic Party. The Senate Majority Leader, Lyndon B. Johnson of Texas, had the support of the South, but was regarded with suspicion by Northern liberals. Then there was the Democratic Party's standard-bearer in 1952 and 1956, Adlai Stevenson of Illinois. Stevenson remained popular among liberal intellectuals, and although he said he would not be an active candidate for his party's nomination in 1960, he left open the possibility that he would run if drafted by the Democratic National Convention.

All of the potential Democratic nominees confronted the public's shock over *Sputnik,* and the feeling that somehow the nation had lost its way. The Soviet satellite's launch contributed to a deep-seated concern in political circles, both liberal and conservative. The United States entered into a prolonged discussion of its "national purpose" during the second term of the Eisenhower administration. A desire to find common ground on key issues such as America's role in the Cold War and how to compete with the Soviet Union drove this search for purpose. Henry R. Luce, the publisher of *Time* magazine, was a leading proponent of the national purpose debate. His publications, including *Time* and *Life* magazines, paid careful attention to the subject. American liberals joined in the discussion, focusing their attention on the need to strengthen America's resolve in the face of the Soviet challenge. According to historian John W. Jeffries, the national purpose debate had important ramifications for the future Kennedy administration. "Rooted in unachieved expectations of the past, the quest for national purpose also pointed ahead to attitudes, directions, and policies of John F. Kennedy's New Frontier."[1]

KENNEDY'S CAMPAIGN SPEECHES

The national purpose debate focused on American anxieties over how the United States was faring in the American-Soviet Cold War. The

goal was to create "will" and "spirit" to fight the Cold War with the Soviet Union among the American public. "What was needed at home,
mostly for effects abroad, was to transcend affluence and revitalize the
American will and spirit, and so turn domestic into global success," according to Jeffries.[2] Jack adopted the search for a national purpose as his
own quest in 1960.

The nation's focus on *Sputnik,* the national purpose, and the alleged
military deficiencies of the United States became a campaign theme
for Jack in 1960. Although the United States possessed nuclear superiority over the Soviet Union, President Dwight Eisenhower did not effectively communicate the real state of affairs to the American people.
Eisenhower's inability to inform the public of the true power relationship
between the two nations opened the door for Jack and others to campaign on the message that the nation had to increase military spending.

Jack seized the issue of the "missile gap," and in his speeches he argued
that the time had come for a Democrat in the White House. He claimed
that the 1960s would be a watershed in world history, a period when the
world balance of power could decisively shift in favor of the Soviets.
"Shocks," he said in one Senate speech, were needed to stimulate change.
It was his hope that the "missile gap" would be the shock to the American public. He hoped that concern over America's military position
would lead the nation to unity and sacrifice. "Four hundred years ago,
the English lost Calais. That event altered the course of British diplomatic history and military policy, and changed the direction of British
public opinion. The acceptance of the loss, and the adjustment of policy,
were not easily or quickly accomplished; but they occurred eventually."
What happened to the British, he said, would happen to the United
States as well. The "missile gap" was comparable to the British loss of
Calais. He hoped that the United States would take advantage of this
"shock." "There is every indication that by 1960 the United States will
have lost its Calais—its superiority in nuclear striking power. If we act
now to prepare for that loss, and if, during the years of the gap, we act
with both courage and prudence, there is no reason why we, too, cannot
successfully emerge from this period more secure than ever." The "missile
gap" was America's Calais because "in the years of the gap, every basic
assumption held by the American people with regard to our military and
foreign policies will be called into question."[3] During a debate in the

U.S. Senate on the "missile gap," Kennedy was asked by a colleague to provide details about the size of the Soviet advantage. Citing an article from the *Washington Post,* Jack said the Soviets would have 500 ICBMs (intercontinental ballistic missiles) by 1960, 1,000 ICBMs by 1961, and 1,500 by 1962. Actually, these numbers were wrong. As president, Jack would never face the number of Soviet missiles he outlined to his Senate colleagues.

Jack pointedly criticized President Eisenhower for leaving the United States vulnerable. "It is unthinkable that we approach the years of the gap with the same sense of normalcy, the same slogans and economics, the same assumptions, tactics, and diplomatic strategy."[4] He thought that during the Eisenhower presidency, the American people had descended into the grips of "complacency." Americans had a tendency, he said, to engage in wishful thinking. This, in turn, led to a predisposition to take the easy way out. The American "national complacency" resulted in a "willingness to confuse the facts as they were with what we hoped they would be." The inability to accept facts "appealed at the same time to those who wanted a quick solution and those who wanted a less burdensome one." Complicating matters, Jack contended, "The people have been misled; the Congress has been misled; and some say with good reason that on occasion the president himself has been misinformed and thus misled."[5] Thus, this young candidate alleged that the five-star general of World War II, who had led the successful D-Day invasion in 1944, was no longer capable of effectively defending the United States. The United States needed new leaders; the leadership of Eisenhower and the Republicans was no longer relevant for the developing "missile gap."

Jack skillfully embraced the missile gap theory. He told campaign audiences that in the early 1960s, the Soviets would possess nuclear superiority because the Eisenhower administration had allowed the Soviets to seize the initiative in the production of ICBMs. As a result, the next American president would face a dangerous expansionist Soviet Union intent on taking advantage of its nuclear superiority. Candidate Kennedy placed President Eisenhower in the role of English prime minister Stanley Baldwin. In doing so, he drew upon his acclaimed study of the growing threat of war in Europe in the 1930s, *Why England Slept*. In much the same way that Baldwin and his successor Neville Chamberlain had misled the British public prior to World War II about the need to rearm in the face of a growing Nazi threat, the Republican administration of Eisenhower, Jack implied, was misleading the American people. "I was in England," he noted, "and saw what happened when Stanley Baldwin went to the people and told them everything was being done in good measure, that the prestige of the British was at its height, that their security was insured. We are not going to have a repetition of that in 1960."[6]

Jack's campaign speeches also emphasized America's international commitments, and how they required sacrifice from the public. He was especially concerned with the need to influence the newly independent nations of Africa and Asia. In this, he criticized the Eisenhower administration for a loss of American prestige that was having a detrimental impact on the geopolitical struggle with the Soviet Union. In other words, he told campaign crowds that the newly independent nations saw the Soviet Union as representing the future, with the United States increasingly relegated to the past. "Why do they think the Soviets are moving faster than we are? Why do people in Africa, Asia, and Latin America begin to wonder whether the Communist system represents the way of the future instead of our system?"[7]

The American people needed a president who would give them a "great goal to believe in" and Jack believed that he was the candidate who could do that. Again drawing upon what he thought British leaders should have done in the 1930s to meet great international challenges, Jack proclaimed, "The next President will confront a task of unparalleled dimensions. But the task will not be his alone. For just as he must offer leadership and demand sacrifices—it is the American people who must be willing to respond to these demands."[8] In a June 1960 speech he said, "it is the American people who must be willing to respond" to presidential direction. The nation was to "voluntarily accept, or reject, the president's 'great goal'." In words that would cause later historians to say that Kennedy was a hard-line anticommunist, as well as someone who reflected the optimism of 1960, Jack said that America could accomplish every objective. The United States "is still capable of building all the defenses we need and all the schools and homes and industries, too—and at the same time helping to build situations of strength and stability throughout the non-Communist world."[9]

Indeed, Jack identified "greatness" with American involvement in international affairs, "I believe that we Americans are ready to be called to greatness." Jack believed that involvement overseas, not isolationism, should be the focus of American foreign policy. Accordingly, presidential attempts to present a "great goal" ought to be built around America's role in the world. He said, "From the lessons we have learned in two world wars, one world depression, and the Cold War, as well as the history of the Republic, the American people will now, I trust, be granted the vision of a new America in a new world. This is the vision without which our people will perish."[10]

In his campaign speeches, Jack referred to the new decade as one of international tension requiring innovation and toughness at home. In discussing the relative decline of the Eisenhower years, he inevitably mentioned the economic performance of the United States. Jack claimed that the American economy was underperforming. The growth rate of the American economy was less than that of its Soviet counterpart. "While our annual average rate of growth was roughly 3 percent, the Russians were up 6 percent," he said in one speech. At the same time that the Soviets were making economic progress, the American people did not realize the extent of the nation's domestic problems. The American public was enjoying a consumer goods buying spree. The people were happy, comfortable, and at ease. The materialism of the Eisenhower years was isolating the American people from the Soviet threat. In one campaign speech, he said: "To meet these urgent responsibilities will take determination, and dedication, and hard work. But I believe that America is ready to move away from self-indulgence to self denial. It will take will and effort. But I believe that America is ready to work. It will take vision and boldness. But I believe that America is still bold."[11]

Though drawing from his own experiences in England and his study of foreign policy while in the House and Senate, many of the ideas expressed by Jack during the campaign regarding presidential power were not his own. In addition to his talented campaign staff that drafted the speeches and articles, Jack was influenced by the prevailing intellectual currents of the day, currents that called for an energetic executive branch. For example, Jack had read and been impressed by *Presidential Power* written by Harvard political scientist Richard Neustadt. Books like Neustadt's characterized Kennedy's era, and they led presidential scholars to adopt the "Savior model" of presidential power. Under this model, scholars saw the presidency as the expression of the national interest and academics, journalists, and presidents themselves called for expanded presidential power. "Strength and the desire to be strong and to show virtue" reflected the main tenets of the "Savior model."[12] In 1960, Jack used his considerable speaking skills to extol the virtues of this model of executive leadership.

THE BATTLE

Joseph P. Kennedy was determined that his second son become the Democratic nominee for president in 1960. As in past elections, Joe avoided any visible activity on behalf of his son. Yet behind the scenes, Joe was constantly making moves to strengthen Jack's case. Not only did he contact prominent Democrats such as Chicago's Mayor Richard Daley but he also made sure that Jack's campaign had the funds necessary for a successful run for the presidency. As he had in the 1952 senate campaign, Bobby became the campaign manager and used his ruthless energy to push his brother and anyone else to their limits. Bobby was a force to be reckoned with by all, including one of the nation's top Democrats and Jack's 1960 vice presidential running mate, Lyndon B. Johnson.

In the years leading up to 1960, Jack was frequently in the company of his trusted aide Theodore C. Sorensen, who accompanied Jack on his many trips across the country. In small towns across the nation, Jack was there meeting with Democratic voters and officials. As a Democratic senator from Massachusetts, Jack had pronounced difficulties in the farm areas of the Midwest, for he had opposed high agricultural price supports, something that was important to Midwest farmers. The Kennedy campaign knew that Jack's votes on agriculture in the Senate would benefit his Midwest opponent, Hubert Humphrey of Minnesota. In the South, Kennedy spent time cultivating political ties with Southern moderates and indeed Jack's votes on civil rights in the Senate were unfriendly to civil rights activists. He clearly tried to maintain a good relationship with Southerners, even though liberals in his party were calling for federal action to end the segregationist policies of the South. Jack's normal tactic in the South was to avoid talking about civil rights when visiting there. Instead, he spoke of the Soviet challenge to the United States, something that was bound to garner him support from largely patriot Southern audiences.

When primary season began in New Hampshire in March 1960, Jack handily won. Being a Northeastern state, New Hampshire was friendly to the Kennedy forces, and thus was not much of a measure for success. That would await the outcome in Wisconsin, a Midwestern state where Humphrey, besides being a senator from the neighboring state of Minnesota, had the support of labor unions. However, the Catholic vote was a big part of the electorate in Wisconsin and so Jack was not without his own base of support there. In addition, Wisconsin's primary was open, meaning that independents and Republicans could vote in the Democratic primary. Therefore, there were diverse elements at play in this primary that made it a must win for Jack in 1960. He had campaigned often in Wisconsin in 1958 and 1959 and was there for most of the six weeks prior to the April 5 vote, standing out in the cold shaking hands with any and all who would listen. Humphrey charged that Jack was no true liberal, and, like his opponents back in 1946, that he was too wealthy to understand the challenges facing ordinary folks. Yet, as they had in the many Massachusetts campaigns, members of the Kennedy family joined in the campaign and were quite effective.

Although Jack captured more than 56 percent of the primary vote, the results were inconclusive. As expected, he won the Roman Catholic vote overwhelmingly. Humphrey won in the more Protestant areas of northern Wisconsin, in an area also influenced by its proximity to Minnesota. Thus, Jack, although victorious, failed to demonstrate that he could win over Protestant voters. His victory, despite the hopes of his campaign, would not be enough to put an end to Humphrey's quest for the nomination. This, in turn, meant that the contest would be decided in West Virginia, an overwhelmingly Protestant state with a reputation for corrupt politics.

The Kennedy campaign poured money into West Virginia. The campaign staff distributed much of the money to Democratic politicians, who would then inform their voters how to vote in the primary. They also gave money to ministers in the state hoping that they could influence their parishioners to vote for Jack. The campaign also produced a slick television documentary that focused on the war hero, and Jack once again brought in his popular family members for campaign appearances. Humphrey, lacking cash, could not match this effort. Although Humphrey did have the support of the United Mineworkers Union, the influence of the union was at its low point. Unemployment among West Virginia miners was high, and so the union was unable to flex its political influence. Humphrey ran a populist campaign, charging that the Kennedys were buying the election. He also played upon the religious prejudices of West Virginians with "Give Me That Old Time Religion" as his campaign song. Baptist ministers raised questions about where Jack's ultimate allegiance would be should he become president, to the people of America or to the pope. Jack worked hard to diminish the concerns about his faith. "Nobody asked me," he said during campaign stops, "if I was a Catholic when I joined the United States Navy. Nobody asked my brother if he was a Catholic or Protestant before he climbed into an American bomber plane to fly his last mission."[13] When the results were counted on primary night, Kennedy crushed Humphrey 60 percent to 40 percent.

Humphrey withdrew from the race, but Johnson, Stevenson, and Symington thought they could still capture the nomination at the Democratic National Convention without having entered any primaries. Although it is true that in 1960, party bosses still controlled the nomination process, the political conventions of both parties existed for television. The idea that Lyndon Johnson could show up, arrange a few backroom deals, and walk away with the Democratic nomination was counter to the public and press perception that the Democratic Convention was to be the "coronation" of Jack as the 1960 nominee. Bobby's highly efficient campaign organization made it certain that the party bosses were going to vote for John F. Kennedy. Although Stevenson, as Jack thought, did announce at the convention his willingness to accept his party's nomination, his offer received few takers. Harry Truman made an appeal designed to weaken Jack and strengthen his preferred candidate, Stuart Symington, but this effort backfired and actually embarrassed the former president.

The selection of Lyndon B. Johnson as Jack's vice presidential running mate remains one of the most contentious elements of the 1960 campaign. Johnson, thinking that Jack had offered him the nomination, accepted and said he would run with him. Bobby, disliking Johnson, went to see him and tried to get Johnson to decline the second spot on the ticket. This action by Bobby angered Johnson and the Speaker of the House, Sam Rayburn (D-TX). Although Jack reassured Johnson that he wanted him to be the vice presidential nominee, the hurt feelings were never repaired. Bobby hated Johnson, and Johnson returned the animosity. Johnson knew that by accepting the vice presidential nomination, he would lose power in Washington. Johnson, as the Senate majority leader, would have much more influence with a President Kennedy than he would as the vice president under Kennedy. As majority leader, Johnson would have major input into the success or failure of Jack's domestic program. As vice president, he would lead no political faction in the Congress, and would have no constitutional responsibilities except performing the largely ceremonial functions of president of the United States Senate. Any duties he might have outside of that role would be determined by President Kennedy. It took the intervention of friend and colleague, Sam Rayburn, to convince Johnson to run with Jack in 1960. Rayburn convinced Johnson that if he had any hopes of running for president he would be better served holding a national office rather than running from the Senate. As Johnson told Clare Booth Luce, the U.S. ambassador to Italy, it is "my only chance ever to be President."[14] Johnson's decision resulted in the so-called Boston-Austin Axis, and his presence on the ticket was probably instrumental for the success of Jack's candidacy in 1960. Northern liberals were outraged by the selection of Johnson by Kennedy. They questioned his liberal credentials and commitment to civil rights. However, his presence on the ticket gave the Democratic Party geographical balance for the forthcoming campaign against Vice President Nixon.

THE GENERAL ELECTION CAMPAIGN

Richard Nixon and John F. Kennedy were relatively young men in 1960. This fact stood out in contrast to the older men who had held the presidency during the recent past: Franklin D. Roosevelt, Harry S. Truman, and Dwight D. Eisenhower. Realizing this, Jack promoted the theme of generational change during the general election campaign. He called for domestic reforms in the tradition of the New Deal of Franklin

Roosevelt and the Fair Deal of Harry Truman, while calling for a more assertive foreign policy, military strength, and rapid buildup of the nation's intercontinental ballistic missiles. He set the tone for the campaign in his acceptance speech at the Democratic National Convention. "The New Frontier is here whether we seek it or not," he told a national audience, "in uncharted areas of science and space, unsolved problems of peace and war, unconquered pockets of ignorance and prejudice, unanswered questions of poverty and surplus."[15] Not wanting the issue of his health to be an issue, Jack's physicians issued statements that he was in excellent condition and did not suffer from Addison's disease. Nixon campaigned on the prosperity and peace of the Eisenhower years, and frequently mentioned the record of the Truman years. Nixon's message was that the United States did not want to return to the economic dislocation of the Truman years and the stalemate in the Korean War that characterized the Truman presidency from 1950–1953.

If 1960 was unusual in having two young candidates for president, it was also unusual in having a Roman Catholic candidate for president. Jack's Catholicism, as it had been in the West Virginia primary, was an issue in the election. The Nixon campaign tried to use the issue against Jack, but not openly. Nixon's campaign enlisted prominent Protestant leaders such as Billy Graham and Norman Vincent Peale in an effort to undermine Jack's popularity. Peale headed the National Conference of Citizens for Religious Freedom, a group of Protestant ministers who raised serious questions about the role of the Catholic faith in the life of the Democratic candidate. The group voiced a number of their concerns in a *New York Times* article on September 8. They questioned a religion that "officially supports a world-wide policy of partial union of church and state wherever it has the power to enforce such a policy." They charged that in some areas of the country "Catholics have seized control of the public schools, staffed them with nun teachers wearing their church garb, and introduced the catechism and practices of their church." Finally, they worried that a Catholic president would not be able to resist the power of the "hierarchy of his church to accede to its policies with respect to foreign relations."[16] Meanwhile, Graham maneuvered behind the scenes by organizing a meeting of prominent anti-Kennedy Protestant leaders in Switzerland. Against the advice of his brother, Lyndon Johnson, and Sam Rayburn, Jack delivered a speech on

September 12 to the Greater Houston Ministerial Alliance in which he addressed the religious issue. He told the assembled 300 clergymen that he believed in "an America where the separation of church and state are absolute." Further, he told them "I do not speak for my church on public matters—and the church does not speak for me."[17] While well received, Jack's speech could not completely eliminate the Catholic issue from the minds of many voters.

THE DEBATES

In 1950, television was a novelty and relatively few American households had one. However, by 1960, 9 out of every 10 households had a television. (Similarly, the Internet was a novelty in the early 1990s, but by the time that Barack Obama was elected president in 2008, the Internet had transformed the way presidential campaigns were conducted.) In 1960, Richard Nixon was clinging to the outdated notions of 1950, that television would not be a major factor in the presidential election. In contrast, Jack was fully aware of the new role of television, and he ably used it in the televised debates of the 1960 election as he had in previous campaigns.

Nixon had a reputation for being an outstanding debater. He had displayed his skills during the 1950s, especially during the "Kitchen Cabinet" debate he had with Nikita Khrushchev in 1959 while on an official visit to the Soviet Union. There were high expectations for Nixon when the two campaigns agreed to debates. While Nixon was confident of his abilities, he nonetheless faced some challenges as the nation's attention focused on the first debate in Chicago, Illinois, on September 26. To begin with, Nixon had been ill, so ill in fact that he had lost a considerable amount of weight. He was still recovering from a leg infection as he and Kennedy gathered for the first debate. In addition, Nixon, for the first debate, refused the use of make-up, something that exaggerated his haggard appearance. Despite these shortcomings, Nixon did perform well in the first debate. Jack's own running mate, Lyndon Johnson, hearing the debate on radio, thought that Jack had lost and Nixon had won. Others who listened to the debate on radio thought likewise. Yet, those who saw the debate on television gave Jack a decisive edge. He appeared calm, vigorous, and prepared. Nixon, on the other hand, slouched, looked quite haggard, and perspired profusely on his cheeks and brow. The contrast was stark. Mayor Richard Daley of Chicago uncharitably said of Nixon, "My God! They've embalmed him before he even died." Henry Cabot Lodge, Nixon's running mate, exclaimed that he had "just lost the election."[18] Ironically, television gave viewers a false image of the candidates. On the question of who was the healthier of the two, Nixon or Kennedy, the answer was clearly Nixon because Jack suffered from a host of afflictions, notably Addison's disease. Nixon had a short-term illness; Kennedy's was long-term and life-threatening. In the presidential politics of the 21st century, a candidate as unhealthy as Jack probably would not have sought the presidency, given today's demand for presidential candidates to release all medical records. But, on television in 1960, Jack looked trim, fit, suntanned, healthy, and full of vitality.

During the first debate, Jack began with his familiar call to "get America moving again." He said the United States was lagging behind the Soviet Union, and that the record of the Eisenhower years could be improved upon under new leadership. Nixon responded by defending the Eisenhower years as one of record economic growth for the United States. In an attempt to link Jack with the last Democratic president, Harry S. Truman, Nixon compared the growth rates of the Truman years with that of the Eisenhower years. Nixon hoped to link Kennedy with Truman because, despite the rehabilitation of Truman's reputation that took place later, in 1960 many Americans still regarded Truman as a failed president; Truman had left the White House in 1953 with a very low public approval number. Although Nixon was ill, he made no major blunders during the debate, a testament to his solid debating credentials. Nevertheless, Nixon lost the war of image on television.

Well aware that he had appeared poorly on television during the first debate, Nixon, who had regained some weight, used make-up during the second encounter. However, appearances were not the main issue of this debate. A foreign policy mistake by Jack placed him on the defense during the October 7 debate. Following the victory of Mao Tse-Tung's Communists in 1949, the Nationalist forces of General Chiang Kai-shek had taken shelter on the island of Taiwan. However, they retained control of the islands of Quemoy and Matsu. The Chinese Nationalists were allies of the United States, and President Eisenhower had pledged to defend those islands from Communist attack. Indeed, in 1954, Eisenhower had staged an impressive naval exercise off the coast of Communist China to demonstrate his willingness to defend these islands. On October 1, Jack had told an interviewer that he did not think it necessary to defend those islands. Therefore, on October 7, Nixon began the debate by attacking Jack's statement. Again invoking the Truman administration's record, Nixon essentially said that the Democrats had lost mainland China to the communists in 1949 while President Eisenhower had defended freedom. Nixon skillfully had portrayed Jack as weak and unwilling to defend freedom from communist aggression.

The third debate on October 13 again focused on Quemoy and Matsu. Nixon was making progress with this line of attack, and Jack

Presidential candidate: For his third presidential debate with Republican candidate Richard M. Nixon, on October 13, 1960, Kennedy spoke from a New York television studio, while Nixon spoke from Los Angeles. (AP Photo/William Smith)

found it hard to deflect the charges. Finally, Jack accused Nixon of a willingness to risk war over two small islands. Jack implied that Nixon was too eager to go to war with Red China. Nixon responded by noting that Jack was advocating appeasement, just as his father had done in the late 1930s when Hitler was demanding territorial adjustments in Europe. Ironically, Nixon had reversed the labels that Jack was using in the campaign against the Eisenhower-Nixon administration. By identifying Jack as Neville Chamberlain, more than eager to surrender territory to the communists in China, Nixon left the Kennedy campaign reeling.

After the debate, Kennedy responded by publicly criticizing the Eisenhower administration for failing to take action against Communist Cuba, 90 miles from the Florida coast. He believed that bringing up the Cuba issue was a valid tactic since Nixon had accused Truman and the Democrats of losing China to the communists. Ironically as a congressman, Jack had attacked the president of his own party, Truman, for doing the very same thing. Jack called for the Eisenhower administration to help Cubans reclaim the freedom of their island—a decision that ignited a controversy lasting long after the 1960 election was over.

In the final debate, Jack placed Nixon in an awkward position. The vice president was aware of plans to train Cuban exiles and land them in Cuba in an effort to overthrow Fidel Castro. Jack called for such an action during the debate. However, Nixon could not admit that he knew of plans to do precisely that. What made Nixon angrier still was his belief that the director of the Central Intelligence Agency, Allen Dulles, had briefed Jack on the plans for Cuba. Nixon felt that Jack was unfairly using against him secret information provided to him because he was the Democratic nominee. Dulles denied having briefed Jack on the details of the proposed action in Cuba, although Jack did have some knowledge of plans through Alabama's Democratic governor John Patterson, who had heard of plans for a clandestine operation against Castro's Cuba. After the election, this plan would be become Jack's first major foreign policy crisis of his presidency, and is known in history as the Bay of Pigs.

Richard Nixon had performed ably during the presidential debates, his poor appearance during the first debate notwithstanding. He placed

Jack on the defensive in the later debates on the issue of China. In all of the debates radio listeners thought he had won the debates. However, the 1960 election had been profoundly influenced by the development of television; and Jack looked presidential on television and Nixon did not.

The televised debate format gained a critical role in presidential campaigns from that point on although the next debate was not held until the 1976 race between Gerald R. Ford and Jimmy Carter. President Lyndon Johnson, the Democratic nominee in 1964, had no need to debate his Republican opponent, Senator Barry Goldwater, given his sizeable advantage in the polls. Moreover, Johnson, who struggled with television, was not keen on replicating the 1960 debate experience. Richard Nixon was the Republican nominee in 1968 and 1972, and he was wary

John F. Kennedy, Jacqueline Kennedy, and their three-year-old daughter, Caroline, shortly after the 1960 presidential election. John Jr. was born two weeks later. The young First Family charmed the nation. (AP Photo)

of the debate format after his encounter with Jack in 1960. However, televised presidential debates have been held ever since.

THE OUTCOME

Jack returned to Massachusetts to await the election returns. Any hope of an early decision was quickly eliminated as the incoming results indicated a close race. It was much closer than Harry Truman's surprise victory in 1948. In fact, the results were so close that Nixon gave some thought to challenging the results. Out of more than 68 million votes cast, Kennedy had defeated Nixon by only 118,574 popular votes. In the Electoral College, Kennedy received 303 votes to Nixon's 219. He won the critical state of Illinois by a few thousand votes. There were charges that Joe Kennedy colluded with either Chicago mayor Daley or gangster Sam Giancana to ensure a positive vote in Chicago. There is no doubt that Daley threw all the resources of his political machine behind the Kennedy campaign, but as biographer Michael O'Brien points out, there "is the lack of evidence of any campaign activity directed by Giancana to elect Kennedy."[19] Regardless, Jack did not need Illinois to win in the Electoral College vote. Although only 38 percent of Protestants voted for him, 78 percent of Roman Catholics did. Clearly, then, the Catholic issue remained problematic for many Protestant voters. Racial politics also played a role. The year 1960 marked the beginning of a trend in which African Americans voted for the Democratic Party in general, and particularly for the Democratic nominee for president. In 1956, Adlai Stevenson received 60 percent of the African American vote. In 1960, Jack received 80 percent. The nation had elected its 35th president, the first Catholic, and one of the youngest presidents in its history.

NOTES

1. John W. Jeffries, "The Quest for National Purpose of 1960," *American Quarterly* 30 (Autumn 1978): 452.

2. Jeffries, "Quest for National Purpose," 452.

3. John F. Kennedy, *The Strategy of Peace* (New York: Harper and Row, 1960), pp. 38–39.

4. Kennedy, *Strategy of Peace*, p. 40.

5. Kennedy, *Strategy of Peace*, p. 40.

6. John F. Kennedy, *Freedom of Communications, Part One: The Speeches, Remarks, Press Conferences and Statements of Senator John F. Kennedy, August 1 through November 7, 1960* (Washington, DC: Government Printing Office, 1960), p. 841.

7. Kennedy, *Freedom of Communications*, p. 456.

8. Kennedy, *Strategy of Peace*, p. x.

9. Kennedy, *Strategy of Peace*, p. 13.

10. Kennedy, *Strategy of Peace*, p. 202.

11. Kennedy, *Freedom of Communications*, p. 21.

12. Erwin C. Hargrove and Michael Nelson, *Presidents, Politics, and Policy* (Baltimore: Johns Hopkins University Press, 1984), p. 7.

13. James N. Giglio, *The Presidency of John F. Kennedy*, 2nd ed. (Lawrence: University Press of Kansas, 2006), p. 17.

14. Robert Dallek, *An Unfinished Life: John F. Kennedy, 1917–1963* (New York: Back Bay Books, 2003), p. 271.

15. Giglio, *Presidency of John F. Kennedy*, p. 17.

16. "Protestant Groups' Statements," *New York Times*, September 8, 1960, p. 25.

17. Dallek, *An Unfinished Life*, pp. 282–284.

18. Dallek, *An Unfinished Life*, pp. 285–286.

19. Michael O'Brien, *Rethinking Kennedy: An Interpretive Biography* (Chicago: Ivan R. Dee, 2009), p. 111.

Chapter 6

INTO THE FIRE:
FOREIGN POLICY

John F. Kennedy entered office at a time of unparalleled tension between the United States and the Soviet Union. During his short tenure as president, the United States faced two nuclear crises with the Soviets, the most important being the Cuban Missile Crisis of October 1962. He also faced challenges in Africa, Asia, Latin America, and the Middle East. Jack was eager to take on the challenges facing the nation. Indeed, as the speeches he delivered on the eve of his inauguration and in the early weeks of his presidency illustrate, he embraced the opportunity to lead in perilous times.

Just before his inauguration as the 35th president, Jack reasserted his campaign messages stating the United States had to project an image of success to the overseas community. Consistent with the practice of previous president-elects returning to their home states to deliver an address to the state legislature prior to the inauguration, Jack seized the opportunity to restate his campaign theme of the historic role of the United States. In his January 9, 1961, address to the Massachusetts state legislature, he pointed out that the world was watching the nation. The international community was looking for signs that the United States was strong and vigorous. In the competition with the Soviet Union, failure at home would harm the nation's position overseas. "For what Pericles said of the Athenians has long been true of this Commonwealth of Massachusetts: 'We do not imitate, but are a model to others'." Placing Massachusetts in an international context, Jack cited the example of John Winthrop, who called upon his fellow colonists to unify behind a sense of mission. "But I have been guided by the standard John Winthrop set before his shipmates on the flagship *Arbella* 331 years ago," he said, "as they, too, faced the task of building a government on a new and perilous frontier. 'We must always consider,' he said, 'that we shall be as a city upon a hill—the eyes of all peoples are upon us'."[1]

Jack carried this theme forward in his inaugural address of January 20, one of the most historic inaugural speeches ever given. The speech famously contains a call for sacrifice: "And so my fellow Americans, ask not what your country can do for you—ask what you can do for your country."[2] Although the address concentrated on foreign policy, it nevertheless had implications for domestic policy. Jack's call for sacrifice was designed to strengthen the United States in international relations. He made clear that he wanted to reduce potential divisions caused by his election. "We observe today not a victory of party," he said, "but a celebration of freedom." National unity, he told the audience at home and abroad, was essential, given the international situation. "Divided, there is little we can do—for we dare not meet a powerful challenge at odds and split asunder." After making his plea for national unity, despite the incredibly close election, he moved on to assert, boldly, America's international obligations: "Let any nation know, whether it wishes us well or ill, that we shall pay any price, bear any burden, meet any hardship, support any friend, oppose any foe to assure the survival and the success of liberty. This we pledge—and more."[3]

In a theme reminiscent of his published senior thesis, Jack said, "In your hands, my fellow citizens, more than mine, will rest the final success or failure of our course." America's global commitments required a citizenry willing to serve and sacrifice for the nation. He reminded his listeners of "the graves of young Americans who answered the call to service surround the globe." However, he argued that the struggle with the Soviet Union would require long-term sacrifice, not the short-term sacrifice characteristic of wartime. The United States was engaged in "a long twilight struggle, year in and year out," which he described as a "burden." This long-term battle would be waged against "tyranny, poverty, disease, and war itself."[4]

Jack did not lament the international struggle, despite the sacrifices that it entailed. On the contrary, he was honored by the role the United States was playing in global politics. "In the long history of the world," he said, "only a few generations have been granted the role of defending freedom in its hour of maximum danger." Therefore, the United States occupied a unique historical position. "I do not shrink from this responsibility—I welcome it. I do not think any of us would exchange places with any other people or any other generation."[5] On other occasions, he would refer to America's far-flung international commitments as "the burden and the glory." In fact, he gathered together a collection of speeches in 1962 and published it as *The Burden and the Glory*. Yet, Jack could have had no idea how much of a burden he would carry as president, ultimately facing a crisis that brought the nation close to a nuclear exchange with the Soviet Union.

BAY OF PIGS AND VIENNA SUMMIT

The new president faced challenges throughout the world, a great many of them centered on the great struggle between the two superpowers, the United States and the Soviet Union. It was a dangerous world, made ever more so by the technological advances in nuclear weapons technology. In 1960, only three nations were nuclear powers: Great Britain, the United States, and the Soviet Union. Yet the world was on the precipice of a nuclear arms race that would begin under Kennedy and not stabilize until the 1970s. On America's southern boundary, the new communist regime of Fidel Castro's Cuba challenged the United States, while in Africa and Asia the superpowers were in a competition for the loyalty and attention of the newly independent countries; in Southeast Asia the United States was allied with the noncommunist, but corrupt, government of South Vietnam; in Europe the unresolved status of Berlin was a major irritant in the American-Soviet relationship. In 1959, an American U-2 spy plane had been shot down over the Soviet Union, raising international tensions, and ruining President Dwight D. Eisenhower's hopes for an agreement with the Soviets. Jack therefore inherited an unstable world, one that could rapidly become more unstable should the rhetoric coming from the Soviet Union become a reality. Just before Jack took office, the Soviet leader, Nikita Khrushchev, delivered his "national liberation speech," in which he said that the newly independent nations of Africa and Asia represented for the Soviets a chance to advance communism. Noting that history was on the Soviet's side, Khrushchev proclaimed that his government would assist national liberation movements around the world, and claimed that it was inevitable that communism would prevail. When Jack read Khrushchev's speech, he was deeply concerned and passed the speech on to his incoming national security team.

Thus, when Jack delivered his inaugural address the audience was both the American people and the Soviet leadership in Moscow. While some viewed his inaugural address as militant, it did contain conciliatory words for Chairman Khrushchev. Indeed, Khrushchev indicated to the American ambassador in Moscow that he would like to meet Jack. Consequently, both sides agreed to a meeting in Vienna, Austria, in 1961, but it would not be a success for the newly elected president.

Before the Vienna meeting ever convened, Jack faced his first foreign policy crisis in Cuba. This small island nation, 90 miles south of Florida, occupied much of Jack's time during his short tenure in office, beginning with a crisis at the Bay of Pigs on the south coast of the island on April 17, 1961. During the Eisenhower administration, the Central Intelligence Agency had developed a plan that called for the United States to train Cuban exiles in Guatemala for an invasion of their homeland. The charismatic Fidel Castro had led a successful revolution that had ousted a repressive regime headed by Fulgencio Batista in 1959. Besides implementing land reforms in Cuba, Castro also seized mines and oil refineries owned by American companies and had developed an ever-closer relationship with the Soviet Union. Khrushchev sent both weapons and military advisors to Cuba. Thus, President Eisenhower approved the planning for an invasion of the island. The assault itself would not trigger the end of Fidel Castro's rule. Rather, the CIA assumed that the news of the invasion would be sufficient to produce public disorder throughout Cuba, and this in turn would lead to Castro's ouster. Although Jack approved the plan, he did so with the proviso that no American military forces could be employed in the endeavor. If the Cuban exiles found themselves in trouble, Jack was not prepared to back them up with American troops. As he said privately, "The minute I land one marine, we're in this thing up to our necks."[6]

Six American bombers flying from Nicaragua, camouflaged as Cuban planes, only destroyed three Cuban planes in air assault. Jack refused to authorize a second air strike. When the 1,400 Cuban exiles landed in Cuba, Castro crushed the invaders with Soviet-made tanks in three days and the hoped-for popular uprising failed to materialize. The disappointing outcome humiliated both Jack and the United States on the world stage. Despite the obvious failure of the plan, Jack's public approval rating increased. Unfortunately for him, the Bay of Pigs occurred just a few months before he was to meet Soviet leader Nikita Khrushchev.

On the way to Vienna, the Kennedys made a stop in France to consult with French president Charles de Gaulle. The two leaders focused their talks on the situation in Berlin, Southeast Asia, and the North Atlantic Treaty Organization. While there were no substantive results from the meetings, the two leaders got along well. On this state visit, however, it was not the president who was the star, but rather America's glamorous and beautiful First Lady. Jacqueline Kennedy had long admired France and French culture. She planned her hairstyle and attire well ahead of the visit to impress the French people. For a banquet at Versailles, for example, she charmed her hosts with a bouffant hairdo and a white Givenchy gown. All of this truly impressed Parisians. It led the president to begin one of his speeches by saying, "I do not think it altogether inappropriate to introduce myself to this audience. I am the man who accompanied Jacqueline Kennedy to Paris, and I have enjoyed it."[7] President de Gaulle was mesmerized by Jacqueline, and throughout Paris, wherever she went, Parisians would exclaim, "*Vive Jacqui*."[8] As *Time* magazine reported, "From the moment of her smiling arrival at Orly Airport, the radiant young First Lady was the Kennedy who really mattered."[9] This pleasant beginning of the trip, however, would be one of its few highlights. The tensions of international politics descended on the American president with a terrifying vengeance.

With the humiliating results of the Bay of Pigs just a few weeks behind him, Jack arrived in Vienna at a disadvantage. Undoubtedly, the

Soviet leader viewed the new president as indecisive and weak. For Nikita Khrushchev, this was a chance to advance his agenda in Berlin. Since the end of World War II, the former German capital had been divided into an Eastern section, under Soviet control, and a Western section, jointly controlled by the United States, Great Britain, and France. For the Soviets and their East German allies, this situation posed a threat to the German Democratic Republic (GDR). Through West Berlin, residents of the GDR were escaping to the pro-Western Federal Republic of Germany. As more and more East Germans moved through West Berlin for more opportunity in the Federal Republic, the economic vitality of the East German communist government was steadily undermined. Simply stated, the Soviets needed to stop the movement of people from the GDR. From the Soviet perspective, the opportunity to deal with a weak and indecisive president over West Berlin was a promising prospect. Khrushchev arrived in Vienna with the objective of testing the president's resolve. He would judge whether Jack Kennedy had the strength to deal with the Soviets over Berlin and other contentious issues. He anticipated that Jack would behave as he had during the Bay of Pigs fiasco.

Khrushchev was not disappointed. On the first day, the president made the mistake of entering into an ideological debate over Marxism-Leninism with Khrushchev even though he had been warned not to do this. Hardly an expert on the ideological system that structured the Soviet Union, Jack engaged in a discussion with a man who was trained in Marxist-Leninist thought. Indeed, Jack angered Khrushchev when he said that the existing balance of power should be maintained to secure peace. Khrushchev recoiled and replied that Jack's suggestion was a prescription for conflict, as Marxism taught that it was inevitable that communism would win the battle with capitalism.

At the end of the day, Jack knew that he had performed poorly. He said of Khrushchev, "He treated me like a boy." American officials were horrified by the president's performance. "There were gasps across town, too," political scientist Richard Reeves has written in his account of the meeting, "as the American team began to go over the minutes of the day's sessions. Kennedy, they realized, had barely defended himself, or U.S. positions."[10]

In the evening, at a palace of the former Austro-Hungarian em-
perors, the two leaders and their wives attended a state dinner. Nina
Khrushchev entered and sat on a sofa, in the location Jack had been sitting. Not realizing this, he almost sat on her lap! Such an embarrassing
incident was representative of the type of day that Jack was having. Yet,
in contrast to the political encounter between Kennedy and Khrushchev, the state dinner proved to be more pleasant. Jacqueline Kennedy
charmed the Soviet leader as she had Charles de Gaulle. Afterward,
Khrushchev sent her a puppy from the dog that had gone into space on
a Soviet space mission. Clearly, the First Lady was having a better time
in Europe than her husband. Yet the pleasantries of the state dinner did
not detract from the tensions that had emerged earlier that day between
the two world leaders. The Soviet leader had quickly formed his opinion of the new American president, "Khrushchev, out at the Soviet ambassador's residence in the suburb of Purkersdorf, told his people: 'He's
very young. . . . not strong enough. Too intelligent and too weak.'"[11]

President Kennedy with Soviet premier Nikita Khrushchev at the Vienna Summit,
June 1961. (John F. Kennedy Library)

When the two leaders met the next day, the conversations centered on the vexing problem of Berlin's status within East Germany, and the tone and substance of Khrushchev's comments were unsettling for the president. Khrushchev boldly told Jack that it was time for a peace treaty with Germany to end World War II officially. He went on to say that the Soviet Union would sign a peace treaty with East Germany by the end of 1961 regardless of what the United States did. Further, he pointed out that if the Soviets signed this peace treaty with East Germany, the Soviet Union would be powerless to prevent the East Germans from seizing West Berlin. This revelation by Khrushchev convinced Jack that the Soviets were going to take action against West Berlin. As biographer James Giglio points out, "For the remainder of the summer the administration concentrated on Berlin, and Kennedy concerned himself about little else."[12]

Khrushchev's behavior in Vienna truly shocked Jack. Although he had been advised prior to the meeting of Khrushchev's threatening and boorish behavior, this did little to comfort the American president. His advisors had told Jack to go along, even have fun with, Khrushchev's antics. They said that was just the personality of the Soviet leader. Yet, Jack couldn't go along or playfully engage the Soviet leader. Those who saw the president following the encounter noted his look of concern about the future. The First Couple stopped in London on the way back home and met Queen Elizabeth II and Prince Phillip. Jack also discussed the Berlin situation with British prime minister Harold Macmillan who thought Jack "seemed rather stunned—baffled perhaps would be fairer."[13] Jack knew that a Soviet or East German move against West Berlin would, given the American pledge to defend the city, likely end in a nuclear war. Despite this, and despite his own feelings of shock over the Vienna meeting, Jack was determined to respond in some meaningful manner.

The president consulted several foreign policy experts, including former secretary of state Dean Acheson, and set up a planning unit within the White House to study options for dealing with Khrushchev's threat to West Berlin. Acheson took by far the most hard-line position on the Soviets. He said that the Soviet posturing over Berlin was simply an effort to gauge the Kennedy administration's willingness to show strength. In the simplest terms, he advised the president to stand up to a bully. To do so, Acheson called for a declaration of a national emergency, and a quick buildup of American military forces, including nuclear weapons. Should Western access to West Berlin be curtailed, he called for the movement of troops through East Germany into West Berlin because these forces would be too strong for the East German military to handle. This would pose a dilemma for Khrushchev: What now? Should I use Soviet troops against the American forces?

While many of Jack's advisors supported Acheson's proposal, including his national security advisor McGeorge Bundy, others were concerned by the risks involved in Acheson's plan for a show of strength. Aides Ted Sorensen and Arthur M. Schlesinger Jr., and the American ambassador in Moscow, Lllewlyn Thompson, were among those who opposed the Acheson proposal. Secretary of State Dean Rusk failed to adopt a clear-cut stance on the matter, a failure to act in a critical situation that caused some in the administration to view him with contempt. By July, Jack had decided against the more provocative proposals of Acheson. He would not declare a national emergency. Nor would he provocatively send American forces against East German troops. He chose, however, to scare the American public. He asked for higher defense spending, an increase in the size of the army, the call-up of reserve units, and directed more attention to civil defense. He urged Americans to take civil defense seriously. This was the era when many Americans built fall-out shelters in their backyards and basements. In a July 25 speech to the American people, Jack said that: "We have another sober responsibility. To recognize the possibility of nuclear war in the missile age, without our citizens knowing what they should do if bombs begin to fall, would be a failure of responsibility." He added that: "In the event of an attack, the lives of those families which are not hit in a nuclear blast and fire can still be saved—if they can be warned to take shelter and if that shelter is available."[14]

Rather than a confrontation, Khrushchev opted to construct a wall sealing off West Berlin from East Berlin. Jack concluded, "It's not a very nice solution but a wall is a hell of a lot better than a war."[15] Although the Berlin Crisis was resolved without it moving to the level of a military confrontation between the two superpowers, the episode left a lasting impact on American-Soviet relations. The president did not challenge the Soviet Union's right to build the wall even though the

Soviet action violated agreements reached in 1945 over the status of Berlin. Because of his success in Berlin, Khrushchev decided to install missiles in Cuba, believing that Kennedy likely would not take military action.

GLOBAL CHALLENGES

Besides his rapidly deteriorating relations with the Soviet Union, Jack faced a host of other foreign policy challenges. Reflecting the concerns he raised about the aspirations for self-determination in the Third World while in the Senate, Jack addressed the rising spirit of nationalism in Africa. (Seventeen nations gained their independence in 1960 alone.) He met with 28 African leaders during his presidency and increased economic assistance to several nations on the continent. Still, he faced innumerable frustrations, including civil strife in the Congo, Soviet inroads into the government of Ghana, Portugal's refusal to grant self-determination in Angola, and his failure to persuade South Africa to relax its apartheid policies.

In the Middle East, Jack pledged to support Israel's right to exist while he sought closer relations with Gamal Abdel Nasser who had merged Egypt with Syria in 1958 to create the United Arab Republic. U.S. relations with the powerful Arab nationalist had deteriorated during the Eisenhower administration. Eisenhower had withdrawn U.S. support for Egypt's Aswan High Dam because of Nasser's purchase of weapons from the Soviet bloc. Jack increased aid to Nasser hoping that it would prompt him to take a more neutral stance in the Cold War, but as in Africa, conditions beyond his control stifled Jack's efforts. Nasser supplied more than 70,000 troops in support of revolutionaries who overthrew the monarchy in nearby Yemen, a decision that prompted conservative Arab nations like Saudi Arabia and Jordan to send aid to the monarchist forces. By the fall of 1963, Jack had to send some U.S. forces to Saudi Arabia to reassure that critical source of Middle East stability.

Jack hoped to improve relations with Latin American nations by making several visits and through his Alliance for Progress. The United States committed to provide $1 billion for the construction of roads, hospitals, and schools in return for pledges of land reform and democratization of the political processes in nations receiving aid. Yet, there were few triumphs. Military coups overthrew some popularly elected presidents, and Jack appeared hypocritical in calling for greater democracy while he opposed left-wing parties like Chile's Popular Action Front.

China and India dominated Jack's attention in Asia. The president saw China as a dangerous expansionist communist power, one eager to develop nuclear weapons. Moreover, his State Department judged Mao Tse-Tung's government as an "unregenerate regime." Because of his own reservations and unanimous opposition to the proposition in the Congress, Jack opposed China's entry into the United Nations. Indeed, in the wake of its border war with India in 1962 and with intelligence that the regime was aggressively pursuing the development of nuclear weapons, Jack considered a U.S. attack to destroy China's nuclear facilities. Jack's relationship with India was much better. While he made little progress in improving relations between India and Pakistan, Jack supported substantial financial assistance to the growing democracy that improved both India's industrial development as well as the president's relationship with Prime Minister Jawaharlal Nehru.

One of Jack's most positive legacies in foreign affairs was his strong support for the Peace Corps. The corps, historian James Giglio has explained, had three goals: "to provide a needed skill to an interested country, to increase the understanding of Americans by other people, and to increase American understanding of other people."[16] During Jack's administration the Peace Corps attracted more than 7,000 volunteers who, after rigorous training on college campuses, served in 44 different nations, most often teaching schoolchildren English. While Jack hoped that the Peace Corps would improve the nation's image in the Cold War, he largely embraced its mission to improve the lives of people in the Third World.

Beyond his struggles with Khrushchev, the situation in Southeast Asia eventually proved to be Jack's biggest foreign policy challenge. When he took office, the tiny nation of Laos was in the midst of a civil war between forces supporting the royal family and the Communist Pathet Lao. Bordered by Vietnam, China, Thailand, and Cambodia, Laos was a key nation in the region. Working through diplomat Averell

Harriman, Jack brokered the establishment of a neutral Laotian government with the Pathet Lao and noncommunists holding cabinet posts. But, it was the war in Vietnam that attracted Jack's greatest attention. As a senator, Jack had consistently criticized the French for their treatment of the people of Indochina and called for the independence of Vietnam. Following the French loss to the Vietminh at Dien Bien Phu in 1954, an international conference in Geneva, Switzerland, had divided Vietnam along the 17th parallel. Ho Chi Minh would rule over a communist North Vietnam and a U.S-backed noncommunist Ngo Dinh Diem headed the government in South Vietnam. The Geneva Accords, however, called for a unification election two years later. The Eisenhower administration backed Diem's decision not to permit the elections and increased financial and military assistance to his regime, which became involved in an escalating battle against North Vietnamese forces that infiltrated into the South.

When Jack took office the multitude of other pressing foreign policy challenges kept him from giving much attention to the conflict in Vietnam until the summer of 1963. His administration had concluded it could best help the Diem regime by providing training of its troops, counterinsurgency forces popularly known as the Green Berets to fight the North Vietnamese guerrilla troops, and funds for infrastructure improvements while seeking to persuade Diem to implement land and political reform. Those efforts had little positive impact on the war effort or in improving Diem's popularity. In the spring and summer of 1963, the Diem government cracked down on Buddhists who protested his policies. The world was shocked by a photo of the self-immolation of a Buddhist priest in Saigon that summer. At that point, Jack's administration made it clear that it would not oppose a coup to topple Diem. In early November a junta of military officers seized Diem and assassinated him.

In the waning days of the Diem regime, Jack began to reconsider the American commitment to the war in Southeast Asia. Only 73 U.S. troops had died in the contest, and the available evidence indicates that Jack was reluctant to risk more lives. An early October meeting of his National Security Council endorsed a recommendation made by Secretary of Defense Robert McNamara and General Maxwell Taylor, one approved by Jack, that called for an increase in the number of U.S.

military advisors in anticipation of the removal of U.S. troops at the end of 1965 and the immediate withdrawal of 1,000 troops in December 1963. His public stance was reflected in an interview with Walter Cronkite on CBS, "We can help them, we can give them equipment, we can send our men . . . as advisers, but they have to win it—the people of Vietnam—against the Communists."[17] Privately, he told people like Senator Mike Mansfield he had to wait until his reelection to end the commitment. What he actually would have done had he not been assassinated is not entirely clear, but many of his close advisors believe he would have indeed drawn down the American commitment to the war. One of his very last statements on the war suggests as much. He told Mike Forrestal, a key State Department official, that he wanted "to organize an in-depth study of every possible option we've got in Vietnam, including how to get out of there. We have to review this whole thing from the bottom to the top."[18]

THE CUBAN MISSILE CRISIS

The American government began to notice the movement of Soviet personnel and equipment into Cuba in July and August 1962. At first, analysts in the CIA thought this was nothing more than a Soviet effort to improve coastal and air defenses. Politically, the Republicans, and some Democrats, were critical of Kennedy's apparent neglect of the situation in Cuba. CIA director John McCone sent a memorandum to the president on August 10, stating that he believed the Soviet Union intended to install nuclear missiles in Cuba. McCone could not persuade the president of that even though he met with Jack on August 29 to reiterate his fears of Soviet intentions. "The Kennedys," according to Thomas Reeves, "who did not entirely trust McCone, thinking him self-serving and extraordinarily hawkish, were inclined to dismiss the warnings."[19] It is important to remember, however, that the CIA had been terribly wrong in the Bay of Pigs incident, so no doubt Jack was suspicious of its intelligence. Yet, these months provided the Soviets a head start on the construction of nuclear bases in Cuba. By the time Jack realized the Soviet threat in Cuba, many in the Soviet leadership doubted the president's willingness to use force to rid the Western Hemisphere of nuclear missiles because he had been ineffectual in his responses to the Berlin Crisis and the building of the Berlin Wall, and had endured the disastrous Vienna summit meeting.

For 13 days in October 1962, the two superpowers faced the prospect of using nuclear weapons in a third world war. On October 14 an American U-2 spy plane retrieved several hundred images of Soviet missile bases being constructed in Cuba. Two days later, the president held his first meeting with advisors over the looming crisis. The president taped the meeting, as he did several others over the course of October. Never before had a government recorded deliberations over whether to go to war! During this initial meeting, Secretary of Defense Robert McNamara identified the central assumption about the Soviet missiles that guided American policy makers during the crisis. "It seems almost impossible to me that they would be ready to fire with nuclear warheads on the site without even a fence around it." "It may not take long," he added, "to place them there, to erect a fence. But at least at the moment there is some reason to believe the warheads aren't present and hence they are not ready to fire."[20] But, the missiles were ready. So, too, were the smaller battlefield support nuclear weapons. Thus, the Kennedy administration's fundamental understanding of the situation was wrong from the beginning. This miscalculation, to draw upon a word that Jack used frequently, almost proved to be deadly. Many of the military options considered by the president during the crisis were based on this assumption.

His superiors had deliberately not informed Anatoly Dobrynin, the Soviet ambassador to the United States, of the placement of nuclear missiles in Cuba. Andrei Gromyko, the Soviet foreign minister, traveled to Washington during the beginning of the crisis and told Jack that the Soviets had no intention of putting missiles in Cuba. Even as he said this, the president already knew that this was a deception. Yet, the administration delayed an announcement of the crisis until a time of its choosing. While the crisis was going on, Jack acted normally, as if there was no crisis in Soviet-American relations. He even campaigned for Democratic candidates for the November mid-term elections, but Jack must have wondered whether the mid-term elections would take place as he knew a nuclear exchange over the impasse was a genuine possibility.

To develop options for him to consider, Jack convened the Executive Committee of the National Security Council (Ex Comm) for the first time on October 16. Ex Comm consisted of high-ranking administration officials from fields that had some connection with the development of foreign policy. That meant that Secretary of State Rusk, National Security Adviser McGeorge Bundy, Secretary of Defense McNamara, Joint Chiefs of Staff chairman General Maxwell Taylor, and Secretary of the Treasury Douglas Dillon were members of Ex Comm. Attorney General Robert Kennedy, the president's brother, was also included. Although the attorney general's office was not directly involved in the making of foreign policy, the president relied upon his brother's insight. Lower-ranking officials, such as undersecretaries, were invited as well. Initially, there was a consensus on the Ex Comm that there should be air strikes against the missile bases in Cuba. Indeed, the president told the group, "We're going to take out these missiles."[21] However, since the Air Force could not guarantee it could remove all of the missiles in such strikes, the advisory group decided that a ground invasion of Cuba would have to follow the air strikes. This early support for the use of air strikes followed by invasion seemed the only viable option. Adlai Stevenson, the American ambassador to the United Nations, had suggested that the president should pursue a diplomatic solution, but Jack dismissed that as an option at the outset.

The American military was keen that air strikes and an invasion be used as the means for removing the missiles and ending the crisis. When they met with the president on October 19, the Joint Chiefs of Staff insisted that this was the most effective means available. General Curtis LeMay, head of the Strategic Air Command, was even willing to use his nuclear bombers against the Soviet Union itself. General LeMay told the president, "I'd emphasize, a little strongly perhaps, that we don't have any choice except direct military action."[22] Jack viewed the opinions of his military commanders with disdain particularly because he believed they had given him bad advice in the preparation of the Bay of Pigs invasion. Further, he believed that the military leaders did not appreciate the difficult political stakes at risk with the situation in Berlin, the possibility that the Soviets might move on Berlin if the United States attacked Cuba. The president emphasized the enormous risks of the Berlin situation to the Joint Chiefs during the October 19 meeting, "There is [always] a chance of their just going in and taking Berlin by force. Which leaves me only one alternative, which is to fire nuclear weapons—which is a hell of an alternative—and begin a nuclear exchange." LeMay countered by dismissing the president's concerns. He said, "I don't think they're going to make any reply if we tell them that the Berlin situation is just like it's always been." If the Soviets did respond, LeMay added, "we're going to fight."[23]

Bobby Kennedy played a key role in the crisis and in Ex Comm. In sentiment, he echoed the views of Undersecretary of State George Ball who opposed a surprise military strike. Bobby feared that history would judge his brother's legacy ill if the United States attacked a small, poor island nation in the Caribbean. True to his reputation, Bobby wanted to be tough with the Soviet Union, but he had doubts about the morality of an American attack against Cuba as the first action by the American administration. Over time, the attorney general became a supporter of a naval blockade of Cuba, with all Soviet ships bound

During the prelude to what became the Cuban Missile Crisis, President Kennedy confers with his brother, Attorney General Robert F. Kennedy, at the White House on October 1, 1962. (AP Photo)

for Cuba boarded, searched, and if necessary turned back, or, if they attempted to run the blockade, then sunk. Under international law, a naval blockade is considered an act of war. Nevertheless, it was not as stark a choice as air strikes followed by invasion, as it did leave open the possibility that the two sides would resolve their differences before it was too late. Ultimately, Ex Comm offered four options to the president: (1) air strikes on military installations in Cuba with warning; (2) air strikes on military installations without warning; (3) full-scale invasion of the island; and (4) a naval quarantine. Implicit with the air strike options was the understanding that an invasion would be necessary to clear the island of nuclear missiles.

On October 20, the National Security Council met and following the president's lead, decided upon a blockade of Cuba, a demand that the Soviet Union remove all offensive missiles from the island, and a planned air strike if Khrushchev refused. When the president briefed congressional leaders on October 22 on his decision not to order an air strike on Cuba and instead order a blockade of the island nation, they expressed opposition. According to Kennedy biographer Michael O'Brien, "Kennedy's prudence annoyed Richard Russell, the crusty, influential Democratic senator from Georgia. A blockade signaled weakness. War with the Soviets would come someday. Would it ever be under more auspicious circumstances?"[24] The Joint Chiefs were particularly unhappy with the president's decision. General LeMay, for example, said that a blockade would be another Munich, another caving in to pressure from an aggressor nation.

Once Jack had reached a decision to employ a naval blockade around Cuba, he knew that he must inform the American people and the world at large about the Soviet missile installations being built in Cuba. Although the press was becoming suspicious that a major international crisis was developing, the Kennedy administration did an excellent job of keeping the crisis a secret. Yet, even as the president prepared to go on national television, the American military buildup in South Florida continued, as many people in the Kennedy administration doubted a blockade would be sufficient to achieve the desired results in Cuba. The president's 17-minute speech on October 22 was stunning. Almost 100 million Americans tuned in. The *New York Times* reported that in cities all across the nation "crowds gathered around taxicabs, in bars and restaurants and in front of their home television sets and radios to listen to the President's talk."[25] Jack told the nation that the Soviet Union had developed a "nuclear strike capability" on Cuba with missiles that could reach many American cities. He explained that the navy would completely quarantine Cuba and prevent the landing of any offensive missiles. Should the Soviets launch any missiles from Cuba as an attack against the United States, he would order "a full retaliatory response upon the Soviet Union." He also pledged to defend West Berlin should the Soviets threaten that city. He demanded that the Soviets remove all offensive weapons and dismantle their missile sites on Cuba.

The naval blockade began on October 24. Originally, it was designed to extend to 800 miles from Cuba, but this was later reduced to 500 miles. Jack hoped that this reduction would not only minimize the chances of a nuclear exchange, but would also give the Soviet Union more time to consider the consequences of its policies and might help Khrushchev in his battles with those inside the Soviet government who wanted a military encounter with the United States.[26] Tensions on the first day were high. But, the blockade was fully operational and virtually the entire American nuclear arsenal was armed and ready to launch an attack against the Soviet Union. Might the Soviets launch a preemptive nuclear strike against the United States? The president apparently thought this was possible. During this time, he requested that Jackie and the children return to Washington where they would be close to nuclear bunkers. In a letter to Jack on October 24, Khrushchev indicated that the Soviet ships would resist the American naval blockade:

> The Soviet Government considers that the violation of the free-dom to use international waters and international air space is an act of aggression which pushes mankind toward the abyss of a world nuclear-missile war. Therefore, the Soviet Government cannot instruct the captains of Soviet vessels bound for Cuba to observe the orders of American naval forces blockading that Is-land. Our instructions to Soviet mariners are to observe strictly the universally accepted norms of navigation in international wa-ters and not to retreat one step from them. And if the American side violates these rules, it must realize what responsibility will

rest upon it in that case. Naturally we will not simply be bystanders with regard to piratical acts by American ships on the high seas. We will then be forced on our part to take the measures we consider necessary and adequate in order to protect our rights. We have everything necessary to do so.[27]

Kennedy's response to this warning and his handling of the crisis generally has been debated for years. Some call it Kennedy's "finest hour" and argue that the president displayed excellent skills at crisis management. While Ex Comm was deliberating the options that might be considered, Jack oftentimes left the meeting. Far from neglecting his duties as president, his action encouraged people to bring up ideas that they might not have otherwise had he been in attendance. Moreover, the absence of the president created a more informal environment. Undersecretaries felt more at ease challenging their superiors during meetings. More important was how Jack reacted to the actions of Khrushchev. On October 26, Khrushchev called on Kennedy to resist the pressures leading the two countries to war, and famously used the analogy of a "knot":

> If you did this as the first step towards the unleashing of war, well then, it is evident that nothing else is left to us but to accept this challenge of yours. If, however, you have not lost your self-control and sensibly conceive what this might lead to, then, Mr. President, we and you ought not now to pull on the ends of the rope in which you have tied the knot of war, because the more the two of us pull, the tighter that knot will be tied. And a moment may come when that knot will be tied so tight that even he who tied it will not have the strength to untie it, and then it will be necessary to cut that knot, and what that would mean is not for me to explain to you, because you yourself understand perfectly of what terrible forces our countries dispose.

He finished the letter by saying:

> Consequently, if there is no intention to tighten that knot and thereby to doom the world to the catastrophe of thermonuclear

war, then let us not only relax the forces pulling on the ends
of the rope, let us take measures to untie that knot. We are ready
for this.[28]

The administration, rather than responding to the hostile message
of October 24, which might have strengthened those in the Soviet
government seeking a confrontation with the United States, decided
to respond to the message of October 26. In this fashion, the United
States simply pretended that the earlier message had never been received. This decision may have saved the world from disaster.

Jack must have identified with Khrushchev's language of the "knot,"
for he was familiar with how previous wars had begun. He had been
reading Barbara Tuchman's recently published *The Guns of August*,
which told the story of the outbreak of World War I in 1914. As scholars
of World War I know, the leaders of all the Great Powers made many
mistakes at the outset of the conflict. Jack was taken with the answer given by German chancellor Theobald von Bethmann-Hollweg
to the question, how did the war begin? His answer: "if we only
knew." One of the difficulties faced by the civilian leaders of 1914 Europe was the transfer of their decision-making power to the military.
Indeed, Jack found it so instructive that he said every American naval
officer should be given a copy of Tuchman's book, and be required to
read it. For example, in 1914, when Russia ordered general mobilization of its army, this removed the ability of Chancellor von Bethmann-
Hollweg to prevent war from breaking out throughout Europe, for the
Russian mobilization automatically meant that Germany would go to
war with France and Russia. In this regard, the German government
had only one military plan, which assumed that it, in order to avoid
a prolonged two-front war on the east and west, would defeat France
first and then move its army to the east to defeat Russia. There was
no other way. Germany could not have simply ordered mobilization,
and stopped there. As soon as Russia mobilized, Germany declared war
on Russia and her army began moving toward France through neutral
Belgium. Germany then made impossible demands of the French, and
when the French refused, declared war on France, which was Russia's
ally. When German troops entered Belgium, Great Britain, which had
guaranteed the neutrality of Belgium, had no choice but to declare war

on Germany. War in 1914 unfolded automatically across Europe, and the civilian authorities lost control to the generals. This historical lesson had a major impact on Jack. Chastened by his reading of the developments in Europe 50 years earlier, Jack said to his staff, "If this planet is ever ravaged by nuclear war—and if the survivors of that devastation can then endure the fire, poison, chaos and catastrophe—I do not want one of those survivors to ask another, 'How did it all happen?' and to receive the incredible reply: 'Ah, if only one knew'."[29]

He was determined that nothing like that would happen in 1962, and that he would not be the Bethmann-Hollweg of 1962, unable to control his military. Accordingly, Jack issued orders that no military action would be taken unless he personally gave the order to fire. Yet, Jack, like Bethmann-Hollweg, faced opposition to this from his military commanders. According to historians Ernest R. May and Philip D. Zelikow, American generals reacted strongly to presidential efforts to contain their power: "President Kennedy passed along a request that special precautions be taken to be sure that, if the Soviets launched a reprisal strike at any point, the Jupiter [nuclear] missiles in Turkey and Italy would not be fired without express presidential authorization. The Chiefs took umbrage at this request and sent back word that they opposed issuing any such special instructions, since doing so would imply lack of confidence in the effectiveness of standing orders."[30]

Despite his orders, war almost broke out in 1962, as it had done in Europe in 1914. Once the naval blockade of Cuba was fully operational, it was the American military, not necessarily the president, who was managing the day-to-day operations of the blockade. The U.S. Navy, like other military organizations, operates according to certain standard operating procedures. When a Soviet submarine got too close to an American destroyer, the commander of the destroyer ordered the dropping of depth charges against the Soviet sub. Clearly, then, Jack was not in charge of the events unfolding on the blockade line. It was a naval commander making the decision to fire. What makes this example of the Cuban Missile Crisis chilling is that, unknown to the American commander of the destroyer, the Soviet submarine was armed with nuclear-tipped torpedoes. As the depth charges were exploding all around the submarine, the Soviet submarine commander's officers were pressuring him to use the nuclear-tipped torpedoes. Not knowing whether war had erupted or not, the Soviet commander, under pressure from his colleagues, was in a difficult position. Had he given in and fired the weapons, World War III would have started, and the president, like the former German chancellor von Bethmann-Hollweg, would have given a similar answer to how it started: "If we only knew."

Throughout the crisis, many, including the president, saw a linkage between the Soviet action in Cuba and the divided city of Berlin. Kennedy feared that Khrushchev had found a way of getting the United States, Britain, and France out of West Berlin. In a telephone conversation with British prime minister Harold Macmillan on October 22, Jack was blunt about Khrushchev's possible reaction to the Cuban crisis, "He could seize Berlin, or he could put on a blockade there, and there are any number of things he could do. We just have to expect that whatever it's going to be it's going to be unpleasant. But I would suspect that he will do something unpleasant to us in Berlin, which I think he is going to do anyway."[31] Clearly, then, if the United States attacked Cuba the Soviets could justify a response against the Western powers in Berlin. Given that the United States had pledged to defend West Berlin, Kennedy knew that should the Soviets move on Berlin a general nuclear war was likely.

October 27 was a dramatic day. Soviet military personnel assumed command of the surface-to-air missile (SAM) sites in Cuba, and a U.S. U-2 spy plane was shot down. Earlier in the day, American planes on reconnaissance were shot at, and one plane had to return to its base because of damage. The downing of the U-2 surprised members of the Ex Comm, as they were discussing ways of communicating a proposed solution of the crisis to Khrushchev. Immediately, they began discussing what this meant for the continuation of intelligence gathering via air over Cuba. This was an important point, as air surveillance was assumed to be the way to delay large-scale air and land operations against Cuba. Without the ability to continue collecting intelligence, air strikes and invasion might become a necessity. Ex Comm members discussed the possibility of launching an immediate air attack against the SAM site responsible for the shooting down of the U-2, but given the time of the day, it would be difficult to do so. General Maxwell Taylor nonetheless urged the president to strike the responsible SAM site "and announce that if any other planes are fired on we will come back and take it."

Perhaps recognizing that the United States was on the verge of World War III with the Soviet Union and the implications of his recommendation, General Taylor said: "They started the shooting."[32]

The potential implications of the U-2 downing became clearer as the group considered what the Soviet action meant in terms of what would be happening two to three days later. Robert McNamara summarized for Ex Comm members and the president what he thought was going to transpire, "We must be in a position to attack quickly. We've been fired on today. We're going to send surveillance aircraft in tomorrow. Those are going to be fired on without question. We're going to respond. You can't do this very long. We're going to lose aircraft. So we must be prepared to attack Cuba quickly." He added, "When we attack Cuba, we are going to have to attack with an all-out attack."[33] Things could not have been more difficult for the president. It appeared that he was about to give orders that would lead to the destruction of much of the world, and the environmental contamination of whatever remained.

Given that the United States had Jupiter nuclear missiles in Turkey on the Soviet border, some of the president's advisors were concerned about what would happen if the Soviets, in response to an American attack in Cuba, attacked the Jupiter missiles. McNamara believed that such an attack would require air attacks by the American and Turkish air forces, using conventional weapons, against targets in the Soviet Union, and against Soviet naval units in the Black Sea. Thus, not only did the Kennedy administration think some sort of action was likely against West Berlin in the event of an American attack on Cuba, but that Turkey also was a likely target. For this reason, McNamara, on October 27, suggested that the nuclear warheads in the Jupiter missiles be removed. This suggestion confused some members. Vice President Lyndon Johnson asked, "Bob, if you're willing to give your missiles in Turkey, you think you ought to defuse them, why don't you say that to him [Khrushchev] and say we're cutting a trade, make the trade there, [and] save all the invasion, lives, and everything else?"[34]

While deliberations continued with Ex Comm, United Nations secretary general U Thant called upon both the United States and the Soviet Union to avoid testing the blockade to permit a diplomatic resolution of the crisis. At the October 25 session of the Security Council at the UN, American ambassador Adlai Stevenson confronted Soviet ambassador Valerian Zorin. When the latter refused to respond to Stevenson's charge that the Soviets had placed offensive missiles in Cuba, Stevenson gained worldwide attention by saying, "I am prepared to wait for my answer until hell freezes over." He then displayed enlarged photographs taken by the U.S. U-2 planes revealing the missile sites. "Our job here," Stevenson proclaimed, "is to save the peace. And if you are ready to try, we are."[35] Meanwhile, the Kennedy administration thought that Khrushchev had sent an offer indirectly to the president. Aleksandr Fomin, the KGB station chief in Washington, met with ABC diplomatic correspondent John Scali to offer a deal that he assumed Scali would relay to the White House. If the United States would pledge not to invade Cuba, the Soviet Union would dismantle the Cuban missile sites and Fidel Castro would pledge to have no more offensive weapons. Scali passed along the offer to Secretary of State Rusk who replied that the United States would be receptive to such an offer. While Fomin was acting unilaterally, his actions foreshadowed an end to the crisis that now featured a large buildup of U.S. forces poised for action. The United States military completed plans for an invasion should the negotiations fail. By October 26, more than 100,000 troops stood ready in Florida as two aircraft carriers headed to Cuba and the Air Force prepared for more than 1,000 sorties.

Finally, Khrushchev contacted the president directly on October 27, outlining a proposal that was more or less accepted by Jack. Khrushchev said, "I therefore make this proposal: We are willing to remove from Cuba the means which you regard as offensive. We are willing to carry this out and to make this pledge in the United Nations. Your representatives will make a declaration to the effect that the United States, for its part, considering the uneasiness and anxiety of the Soviet State, will remove its analogous means from Turkey. Let us reach agreement as to the period of time needed by you and by us to bring this about."[36] Jack drafted a response indicating that he would end the blockade and not invade Cuba if the Soviets would remove their missiles. Bobby Kennedy took the offer to a meeting with Ambassador Dobrynin who insisted that the United States would have to remove its missiles in Turkey. The attorney general agreed, with the understanding that that element of the arrangement would remain secret.

Thus, it appeared to the American public that Jack had "won" the Cuban Missile Crisis. Perhaps this public perception of an American victory contributed to the strong Democratic performance in the November 1962 mid-term elections. Yet, the lasting significance of the crisis may be in the manner in which the two superpowers conducted their relationship for the remainder of the 20th century. While the Cold War continued, the nuclear relationship between the two countries became more stable. The prospect of a nuclear exchange led the two governments to take immediate action to improve their relations. Following the Cuban Missile Crisis, the two nations agreed that there needed to be a "hotline" between Washington and Moscow so that the two governments could communicate in case of a crisis. Portrayed as a "red phone" in the Oval Office by many Hollywood movies, this link was instead a teletype machine in which printed messages could be sent from one government to another. In the final analysis, no one "won" the Cuban Missile Crisis. It was plain old-fashioned luck that the world escaped disaster in the fall of 1962. Some analysts have argued that if Jack had performed more effectively in other foreign crises prior to the Cuban Missile Crisis, perhaps he would have felt less the need to be "firm" with Khrushchev in what turned out to be the most dangerous moment of the 20th century. The president who used fear in domestic politics, ultimately frightened himself, according to political scientist Bruce Miroff, "The comparison of Kennedy at the beginning of the crisis and at its end produces a surprise twist—a climax that had been concealed by the original accounts of the triumphant American hero. It shows us the bold risk taker at the outset of the crisis turning into a frightened, cautious, and ultimately more admirable figure at its end."[37]

AFTER THE MISSILE CRISIS

Jack emerged as an enlightened leader in a nuclear age. In his commencement address at American University in 1963, he noted that no society is so evil that it deserves annihilation. All individuals, whether Soviet or American, are mortal. He said we share one planet. The Kennedy administration became the first U.S. administration to sign an arms control agreement with the Soviet Union. The Test Ban Treaty of

President Kennedy signs the Nuclear Test Ban Treaty, October 7,
1963. (Courtesy Robert Knudsen, White House/John F.
Kennedy Presidential Library)

1963 was a watershed event in American-Soviet relations. Both countries pledged to end the atmospheric testing of nuclear weapons.

In the summer of 1963, Jack made a memorable trip to Europe. In
West Berlin, he delivered one of the most famous speeches of his presidency, the "Ich bin ein Berliner" address. He made the trip to West
Berlin to show solidarity with the residents of the city who had been
through so much since 1961: the threat of war, the construction of the
Berlin Wall, and the city's precarious position during the Cuban Missile
Crisis. Accompanied by West Berlin mayor Willy Brandt and German
chancellor Konrad Adenauer, the president proudly exclaimed, "All
free men, wherever they may live, are citizens of Berlin, and therefore,
as a free man I take pride in the words 'Ich bin ein Berliner'."[38] The
crowd was enthusiastic. Jack, appearing vigorous and certainly young,
projected to a Europe still emerging from the shadows of World War II
the image of a young, energetic United States and to many around the
globe he projected the image of a statesman.

NOTES

1. Address of President-Elect John F. Kennedy Delivered to a Joint Convention of the General Court of the Commonwealth of Massachusetts, January 9, 1961, John F. Kennedy Presidential Library and Museum, http://www.jfklibrary.org/Historical+Resources/archives/Reference+Desk/Speeches/JFK (accessed September 30, 2010).

2. *Public Papers of the Presidents of the United States: John F. Kennedy, 1961* (Washington, DC: Government Printing Office, 1962), p. 3.

3. *Public Papers* (1962), p. 1.

4. *Public Papers* (1962), p. 2.

5. *Public Papers* (1962), p. 2.

6. Jeremy Isaacs and Taylor Downing, *Cold War: An Illustrated History, 1945–1991* (Boston: Little, Brown, 1998), p. 188.

7. Robert Dallek, *An Unfinished Life: John F. Kennedy, 1917–1963* (New York: Back Bay Books, 2003), p. 400.

8. Donald Spoto, *Jacqueline Bouvier Kennedy Onassis: A Life* (New York: St. Martin's Press, 2000), p. 180.

9. Thomas C. Reeves, *A Question of Character: A Life of John F. Kennedy* (New York: Free Press, 1991), p. 298.

10. Richard Reeves, *President Kennedy: Profile of Power* (New York: Touchstone, 1993), p. 166.

11. Richard Reeves, *President Kennedy*, p. 166.

12. James N. Giglio, *The Presidency of John F. Kennedy*, 2nd ed. (Lawrence: University Press of Kansas, 2006), p. 78.

13. Isaacs and Downing, *Cold War*, p. 173.

14. *Public Papers* (1962), p. 536.

15. *Public Papers* (1962), p. 182.

16. Giglio, *Presidency of John F. Kennedy*, p. 156.

17. Giglio, *Presidency of John F. Kennedy*, p. 266.

18. Dallek, *An Unfinished Life*, pp. 685–686.

19. Thomas C. Reeves, *Question of Character*, p. 366.

20. Ernest R. May and Philip D. Zelikow, eds., *The Kennedy Tapes: Inside the White House during the Cuban Missile Crisis* (Cambridge, MA: Belknap Press of Harvard University Press, 1997), p. 49.

21. Dallek, *An Unfinished Life*, p. 547.

22. May and Zelikow, *Kennedy Tapes*, p. 177.

23. May and Zelikow, *Kennedy Tapes*, pp. 176 and 178.

24. Michael O'Brien, *John Kennedy: A Biography* (New York: Thomas Dunne Books, 2005), p. 666.

25. "Cuba Action Gets Public's Backing," *New York Times*, October 23, 1962, p. 21.

26. Many years later, Yugoslavian communist leaders told American diplomat and writer George F. Kennan that Khrushchev had placed the missiles in Cuba to satisfy the hard-line elements within the Soviet government. See Thomas C. Reeves, *Question of Character*, p. 365.

27. Letter from Chairman Khrushchev to President Kennedy, October 24, 1962, Kennedy-Khrushchev Exchanges, State Department, http://www.state.gov/www/about_state/history/volume_vi/exchanges.html (accessed June 16, 2010).

28. National Security Files, Countries Series, USSR, Khrushchev Correspondence. Secret; Eyes Only; Niact; Verbatim Text. Passed to the White House at 9:15 P.M., October 26, 1962, John F. Kennedy Library.

29. Dallek, *An Unfinished Life*, p. 505.

30. May and Zelikow, *Kennedy Tapes*, p. 213.

31. May and Zelikow, *Kennedy Tapes*, p. 284.

32. May and Zelikow, *Kennedy Tapes*, pp. 572 and 574.

33. May and Zelikow, *Kennedy Tapes*, p. 581.

34. May and Zelikow, *Kennedy Tapes*, p. 582.

35. Isaacs and Downing, *Cold War*, p. 198.

36. Letter from Chairman Khrushchev to President Kennedy, October 27, 1962, Kennedy-Khrushchev Exchanges, State Department, http://history.state.gov//historicaldocuments/frus1961-63v06/d66 (accessed June 16, 2010).

37. Bruce Miroff, *Icons of Democracy: American Leaders as Heroes, Aristocrats, Dissenters, and Democrats* (New York: Basic Books, 1993), p. 288.

38. Richard Reeves, *President Kennedy*, p. 536.

Chapter 7

THE NEW FRONTIER: DOMESTIC POLICY

John F. Kennedy ran as a liberal in the tradition of Franklin D. Roosevelt and Harry Truman. He advocated national health insurance for the elderly, what would eventually become Medicare; more federal funding of elementary, secondary, and higher education; raising the minimum wage; establishing a housing department; housing legislation; economic help for depressed areas; and an aggressive space program. His greatest domestic challenge, however, was how best to respond to the growing demands for civil rights.

CIVIL RIGHTS

When Jack became the 35th president, few could have anticipated that civil rights would become the issue that defined the 1960s. The various reform efforts of Booker T. Washington, Ida B. Wells, W.E.B. Du Bois, Marcus Garvey, and A. Philip Randolph had led to only modest gains in the struggle against discrimination and racial segregation. The U.S. Supreme Court decision in the *Brown v. the Board of Education of Topeka* case in 1954 represented the nation's highest court's challenge to the long-accepted doctrine of "separate but equal" and began the painfully slow process of ending racial segregation in American schools. A year later, Rosa Parks's refusal to give up her seat to a white man on a Montgomery, Alabama, bus led to the successful Montgomery Bus Boycott, the emergence of Dr. Martin Luther King Jr. as a national figure, and introduced nonviolent resistance as an approach to fight injustice. Yet, it would take presidential initiative and time to change the ways of a deeply segregated land. Initially, Jack's stance was practical. He wanted to retain the support of Southern whites, while not endangering his support among Northern liberals and blacks who favored an aggressive civil rights policy. Historian Carl Brauer has written that after Jack became president, members of his administration refrained from describing civil rights in moral terms although they were more than willing to mention the negative impact of Southern racism on America's international standing. "Repeatedly," Brauer has written, "the Kennedys and members of the administration placed their comments in an international context."[1]

Civil right advocates had reason to doubt Jack's commitment to reform. He maintained close ties with Southern Democrats, including Alabama governor John Patterson, Arkansas senator J. William Fulbright, and North Carolina governor Luther Hodges. In fact, Jack's voting record on civil rights in the Congress was at best middle-of-the-road. His moderation was best reflected in his voting record on the Civil Rights Act of 1957, which Majority Leader Lyndon Johnson had shepherded through the Senate. On this bill, Jack supported amendments that weakened the legislation advocated by Southern Democrats, and he opposed liberal attempts to bypass the Senate Judiciary Committee, chaired by Senator James Eastland of Mississippi, a strong segregationist and one who could damage any civil rights bill considered by the Congress.

During the Senate debate over the bill, Jack did refer to the proposed legislation as "a turning point in American social and political thought." The nation, he said, had to consider the bill in view of the American-Soviet Cold War. The Civil Rights Act, he said, "represents an almost universal acknowledgment that we cannot continue to command the respect of peoples everywhere while we ignore" the civil rights problem at home.[2] At the same time that he argued that America must demonstrate a commitment to its highest ideals, Jack's remarks in the

Senate displayed deference to his Southern colleagues. He emphasized a gradual approach to social change in the South out of his sense that national unity must be maintained given the ideological confrontation with the Soviet Union. Although he did not say so explicitly, he must have had some fear that incidents like the Montgomery Bus Boycott and the burgeoning civil rights movement led by Martin Luther King Jr. threatened the unity of the nation. After all, it would have been nearly impossible to satisfy white Southerners, on the one hand, and African Americans, on the other, without triggering domestic unrest. During the Senate debate on August 1, 1957, as others questioned whether all-white juries in the South would be able to faithfully enforce the legislation, Jack said that he thought they could. "I do not count myself," he explained, "among those who are cynical about the capacity of citizens in any section of the country to rise to the challenge of one of the highest responsibilities of freemen—the preservation of law and of a just social order."[3]

As a presidential candidate, Jack continued his deferential treatment of the South. In campaign stops throughout the region, he presented his thoughts on race with an acknowledgment that many white Southerners would challenge his views, "but at least," he said, "I have not changed that view in an election year, or according to where I am." On the infrequent campaign stops that he mentioned civil rights in his speeches, Jack balanced it with praise for Southern heritage and culture. In South Carolina, for example, he paid tribute to John C. Calhoun, placing him alongside "the spirit of our great Democratic leaders, from Jefferson and Jackson to Roosevelt and Truman."[4] At other campaign stops in the South, he paid tribute to the committee chairmen of the Congress, many of whom had played a role in defeating, or slowing down, civil rights legislation.

One of the leading civil rights issues during the Kennedy years was desegregation of housing. As a presidential candidate in appearances before Northern liberals and civil rights advocates, Jack had promised to sign an executive order "at the stroke of a pen" desegregating housing. However, as president he delayed any action on the matter. As always, his primary concern was with maintaining good relations with Southern Democrats. He believed that an executive order on housing would harm other elements of his legislative program. Eventually, civil rights

activists organized a "pens for Jack" campaign with a considerable
number of ink pens being sent to the White House! On November 20,
1962, after the mid-term elections had returned Democratic majorities
to the Congress, Jack finally signed an executive order desegregating
federally owned and financed housing. Following a consistent strategy,
he avoided investing civil rights with a moral emphasis. Little fanfare
accompanied his announcement of the executive order at a press conference.

Similarly, Jack's September 30, 1962, televised address to the nation concerning the admission of James Meredith to the University of
Mississippi clearly reflected his cautious approach to civil rights. He,
as President Dwight Eisenhower had done in the integration of Central High School in Little Rock, Arkansas, five years earlier, stressed
his legal responsibilities as president. Instead of describing Meredith's
admission as a moral issue, he discussed the need for citizens to obey the
law. "Our nation is founded on the principle that observance of law is
the eternal safeguard of liberty and the defiance of the law is the sur-
est road to tyranny," he said.[5] Even if the law is objectionable, citizens
have a responsibility to respect and obey the requirements of the law.
In compelling the state of Mississippi to permit Meredith's admission
to the university, the president said that he was fulfilling the legal "obligation" of the federal government. In fact, Jack explained that he only
reluctantly intervened in the case, saying, "I deeply regret the fact that
any action by the Executive Branch was necessary in this case." Following a federal court order, obtained by the NAACP for Meredith's admission, Jack had to ensure that the state of Mississippi was compliant. As
he explained, "Even though this government had not originally been a
party to the case, my responsibility as President was therefore inescap-
able. I accept it. My obligation under the Constitution and statutes of
the United States was and is to implement the orders of the court with
as little force and civil disorder as the circumstances permit."[6] He made
such a cautious statement because he faced a staunch segregationist
governor named Ross Barnett who at one point told Attorney General
Bobby Kennedy, "I won't agree to let that boy get to Ole Miss. I will
never agree to that. I would rather spend the rest of my life in a peniten-
tiary than do that."[7] Jack had his administration work behind the scenes
on Meredith's behalf. He also made several personal calls to Barnett,

but ultimately had to use the threat of reducing federal appropriations to Mississippi and had to dispatch both deputy marshals and military police to put down a riot on the Oxford, Mississippi, campus. To this point in his presidency, it is clear that Ted Sorensen's characterization of Jack's approach to civil rights in his congressional days remained true as president. Political expediency still largely shaped his approach.

A year later, however, on June 11, 1963, Jack delivered the most important speech on civil rights of his presidency. In this address, he finally publicly embraced civil rights as a "moral issue." He replaced his past reticence with a new passionate appeal for change, an effort to link social change with patriotism. "No one has been barred," he said, "on account of his race from fighting or dying for America—there are no 'white' or 'colored' signs on the foxholes or graveyards of battle."[8] Indeed, he issued a call for activism. "Listening to his talk by shortwave, I felt a thrill run down my back," Harris Wofford, the administration's special assistant on civil rights, observed.[9] The context for this speech explains his change in attitude toward the imperative of civil rights reform.

The address followed the aftermath of the Birmingham, Alabama, crisis and the confrontation with Alabama governor George Wallace over the admission of black students at the University of Alabama. In early May 1963, the Southern Christian Leadership Conference, Martin Luther King Jr., and a local minister named Fred Shuttlesworth had led peaceful efforts to desegregate public facilities and challenge discriminatory hiring practices in Birmingham. The city's police department, headed by Eugene "Bull" Connor, used dogs and fire hoses against peaceful demonstrators. The scenes from Birmingham, broadcast on national television, shocked Jack and the nation. Seeing the photos of the police dogs attacking young demonstrators, the president remarked, "It makes me sick."[10] Besides Birmingham, there were significant demonstrations against segregation in Jackson, Mississippi, and Baton Rouge, Louisiana. These events drew considerable interest in the media. NBC aired a three-hour documentary on the civil rights movement, and *Time* magazine addressed "The Negro Revolt." In the face of this extraordinary resistance to integration and the media coverage it attracted, Kennedy concluded, "The people in the South haven't done anything about integration for a hundred years, and when an outsider intervenes, they tell him to get out; they'll take care of it themselves, which they won't."[11] When Jack consulted with Vice President Lyndon Johnson, the Texan told the president, "the Negroes are tired of this patient stuff and tired of this piecemeal stuff and what they want more than anything else is not an executive order or legislation, they want a moral commitment." He urged the president to make a national television address to deal with this escalating challenge and say "We give you a moral commitment. The government is behind you. You're not going to have to do it in the streets. You can do it in the courthouses and the Congress."[12]

The following month, Governor Wallace was ready to make good on a pledge he had made a few months earlier, "Segregation now! Segregation tomorrow! Segregation forever!," by attempting to prevent the admission of two black students, Vivian Moore and James Hood, at the University of Alabama. On June 11, he stood in the doorway of the administration building and forced Deputy Attorney General Nicholas Katzenbach to order him to stand aside and permit the admission of the two students.

Jack chose this moment, the evening of June 11, to address the American people announcing that he would push for a comprehensive civil rights law. He began his speech with a summary of the events at the university. "The presence of Alabama National Guardsmen was required at the University of Alabama," he said, in order to "carry out the final and unequivocal order" of the courts. Jack then called on white Americans to reexamine their attitudes toward race relations. "I hope that every American, regardless of where he lives, will stop and examine his conscience about this and related incidents." The United States was founded on the principle of equality. Given the diverse nature of the American people, Americans should move beyond past attitudes about race: "This nation," he reminded the television audience, "was founded by men of many nations and backgrounds. It was founded on the principle that all men are created equal, and that the rights of every man are diminished when the rights of one man are threatened."[13] Clearly, Jack presented this as a national problem and a historic legacy that had to be overcome. "This is not a sectional issue," he said, adding that "difficulties over segregation and discrimination exist in every city, in every state of the Union, producing in many cities a rising tide of discontent."

Drawing upon the efforts of Abraham Lincoln, he said that it was time to finally include black Americans in the national life of the United States. "One hundred years of delay have passed since President Lincoln freed the slaves, yet their heirs, their grandsons, are not yet free. They are not freed from the bonds of injustice. They are not yet freed from social and economic oppression, and this nation, for all its boasts, will not be fully free until all its citizens are free."[14] The economic inequality of black Americans formed a key part of his address. Jack described the plight of black Americans as no other president had ever done. "The Negro baby born in America today, regardless of the section of the Nation in which he is born, has about one-half as much chance of completing high school as a white baby born in the same place on the same day, one-third as much chance of completing college, one-third as much chance of becoming a professional man, twice as much chance of becoming unemployed, about one-seventh as much chance of earning $10,000 a year, a life expectancy which is 7 years shorter, and the prospect of earning only half as much."[15] Jack then delivered the most memorable part of his June 1963 speech: "We are confronted primarily with a moral issue. It is as old as the scriptures and is as clear as the American Constitution."

Jack's previous policy of maximum executive action, minimum legislative action was no longer appropriate for circumstances following Birmingham and the crisis at the University of Alabama. "Next week I shall ask the Congress of the United States to act, to make a commitment it has not fully made in this century." That "commitment" was "the proposition that race has no place in American life or law." Specifically, Kennedy requested legislation that struck at the heart of the South's system of segregated facilities. He wanted to end the practice that kept black Americans from eating at restaurants, checking into a hotel, or seeing a movie. "I am, therefore, asking the Congress to enact legislation giving all Americans the right to be served in facilities which are open to the public—hotels, restaurants, theaters, retail stores, and similar establishments."[16]

The president's civil rights proposal was a dramatic departure. It was a direct attack on the South's system of segregated facilities. The news coverage from Washington of his decision was favorable. Political commentator Walter Lippman said "no President has ever done this before, none has staked his personal prestige and has brought to bear all the powers of the Presidency on the Negro cause." However, it was the president's decision to move forward aggressively on civil rights. As a New Englander and as one who had observed the brutality of some white Southerners during his administration, the president was puzzled. In a candid remark to aide Arthur Schlesinger Jr., Jack said, "I don't understand the South."[17]

As political scientist Irving Bernstein has observed, "A hot summer was about to begin," and "it was indispensable, the President thought, to get blacks off the streets and into the courts," where more challenges to racial discrimination could be made.[18] "The Kennedy commitment was designed to preserve the fabric of our social order," Jack's aide Ted Sorensen explained. According to him, the new Kennedy policy was designed "to prevent the unsatisfied grievances of an entire race from rending that fabric in two."[19] Nonetheless, Jack worried that pushing civil rights legislation could cost him the 1964 election because he would

On August 28, 1963, President Kennedy met with leaders of the March on Washington. From left, Whitney Young, Dr. Martin Luther King Jr., John Lewis, Rabbi Joachim Prinz, Dr. Eugene P. Donnaly, A. Philip Randolph, President Kennedy, Walter Reuther, Vice President Lyndon B. Johnson (rear), and Roy Wilkins. (AP Photo)

alienate Southern voters. Moreover, he sought to discourage the soon-to-be-famous August 28 March on Washington, fearing it would hurt the chances for his comprehensive civil rights bill in Congress, one that would guarantee equal access to public accommodations, provide greater protection of voting rights, and would expand the powers of the Justice Department to enforce federally court-ordered desegregation. He told civil rights activists like Dr. King, A. Philip Randolph, Roy Wilkins, and Whitney Young, "We want success in the Congress, not a big show on the Capitol."[20] Jack did not live to see his civil rights proposal enacted into law. President Lyndon Johnson signed the Civil Rights Act into law on July 2, 1964, a little over a year after Jack's historic speech. Despite that, his embrace of reform in the summer of 1963 was a significant moment in American history, a lasting legacy from the Kennedy presidency.

THE NEW FRONTIER

In the 1960 Democratic nominating convention, Jack had told the American people that they faced a "New Frontier," an opportunity to pursue national greatness and the public interest. His vision for that new frontier beyond advancing the cause of equal rights included improvements in education funding, aid to regions of the country facing chronic economic difficulties, health care for the aged, and a vigorous space program. However, like President Harry Truman, Jack faced a Congress hostile to most of these liberal reform proposals. Truman, too, had tried to secure passage of Medicare for seniors but had faced opposition from Republicans and conservative Southern Democrats. This coalition was still in place in 1961. Moreover, Jack's ability to pass legislation was hampered by Vice President Johnson's new role in the executive branch. During the 1950s, Johnson had been an effective majority leader of the Senate Democrats forging coalitions between conservatives and liberals, Republicans and Democrats. Johnson's replacement as majority leader, Senator Mike Mansfield of Montana, lacked Johnson's legislative abilities. Then, too, Speaker of the House Sam Rayburn was in poor health as Jack began his presidency and would be dead by the fall of 1961. His replacement, Congressman John McCormack of Massachusetts, had a strained relationship with Jack because of long-standing political disagreements within the Massachusetts Democratic

Party, including Jack's refusal to join McCormack and other members of the Massachusetts delegation in pushing for a commutation of Boston mayor James Michael Curley's sentence for mail fraud in 1947.

Nonetheless, Jack quickly sought to implement his reform ideas, enjoying some successes in 1961 and 1962. In February 1961, he proposed legislation to raise the minimum wage from $1 to $1.25 an hour. The bill immediately encountered opposition from Southern Democrats and Republicans who said the wage increase was too high. Moreover, Southern conservatives sought to exempt laundry workers, many of them black women from the South, from the proposed hike in minimum wage. After much struggle, Jack was able to sign into law an increase. Although it exempted about 500,000 workers including laundry workers, more than 3.5 million saw their wages go up. Stunned by the poverty he witnessed campaigning in West Virginia, Jack pushed successfully for legislation to create an Area Redevelopment Administration with funding for industrial development and job training largely in the South, a program that eventually created more than 25,000 jobs. In 1962, he gained approval of the Manpower Development and Training Act, which also provided funds for job training. Finally, he won passage of a nearly $5 billion Housing Act in 1961, which funded public housing for low-income families, low-interest loans for middle-class Americans to buy homes, and some mass transit facilities.

However, the administration suffered several setbacks including a proposal for education funding that faced opposition from Democratic and Republican conservative forces as well as from Catholic members of Congress. Catholic Democrats, many from the North and inclined to support education funding, objected to any proposal that did not provide funding for parochial schools. Without the support of Northern Catholic Democrats Jack's February 1961 proposal for the use of federal money to finance construction at public schools had no chance of success in the Congress. The administration introduced legislation in February 1961 that would have provided funding for teachers' salaries and construction at public schools as well as construction loans to parochial schools. Jack lost this battle as the conservatives of both parties and Catholic Democrats voted no.

Jack's biggest defeat was Medicare, a plan for national health insurance for elderly Americans. Throughout the 20th century, there had been calls for a national health insurance plan. Republican Theodore Roosevelt had first proposed national health insurance for all Americans in 1912. Despite this, nothing had been done. The American Medical Association, the professional organization for the nation's doctors, had been steadfast in its opposition to any reform since the days of Roosevelt's proposal, warning Americans about the perils of "socialized medicine." The fundamental problem was insurance companies' refusal to issue health policies to older Americans, even if they were able to afford the costly premiums. Yet, on the eve of Jack's candidacy for president, public opinion polls indicated that support for public health insurance for the elderly had gained support because of escalating health care costs. As political scientist Irving Bernstein has explained, "By the spring of 1960 health care under Social Security was probably the hottest issue of the gathering presidential campaign."[21] The blueprint for Medicare was a plan introduced by Jack and three other liberals on May 6, 1960. Under its provisions, there would be 90 days of hospital coverage, 180 days of coverage in a nursing home, and 240 days of home health care.

Once Jack became president, the chances of success with Medicare in the Congress were limited. There were competing plans in the Congress, and the American Medical Association continued its strong opposition to any health bill. Making matters worse, the House Ways and Means Committee, which held jurisdiction over Medicare, was chaired by Wilbur Mills of Arkansas, a Southern Democrat opposed to the Medicare legislation. Mills did agree to schedule a hearing on Medicare, but would not allow a vote to proceed. At the time, committee chairmen held the power to determine when or if a bill would receive a vote. Early in 1962, Kennedy held a rally in support of the proposal at Madison Square Garden in New York with an estimated 20,000 people in attendance and with all three television networks covering the event. Unfortunately for supporters of Medicare, Jack performed poorly in his speech. As Irving Bernstein claimed, "It may have been the worst speech Kennedy ever made. He disliked the address that had been written for him, tried to make some last minute notes, and then decided to speak extemporaraneously."[22] Congressional Democratic leaders decided the best strategy was for the Senate to attach Medicare as an amendment to a welfare bill being sent to it by the House, and hope that, should the Senate vote affirmatively, they could negotiate a deal for Medicare with the House in a conference committee. That plan ended on July 17, 1962, when the Senate rejected the plan 52–48.

Although Jack gave up hope for any positive legislative action on health care for seniors, Medicare became law on July 30, 1965 as President Johnson signed the Social Security Act of 1965, which added Medicare to the original Social Security Act signed by President Franklin Roosevelt 30 years earlier. President Truman, who had called for national health insurance during his presidency, sat with Johnson at the signing ceremony.

THE NEW ECONOMICS

The business community viewed the Kennedy administration with suspicion even though his policies were in fact favorable to American business, and despite the fact that a number of high-ranking Kennedy officials were from the business world. Part of the mistrust stemmed from the business community's historic fears of Democratic presidents dating back to Franklin Roosevelt. Yet, Jack named a number of business leaders to the cabinet: Douglas Dillon, a former investment banker; J. Edward Grey, an executive with Prudential Insurance; Luther Hodges, a textile executive from North Carolina; and Robert McNamara, president of the Ford Motor Company. In addition, Jack's father had been a highly successful Wall Street investor.

Despite his background, Secretary of Commerce Hodges got the administration's relationship with business off to a poor start. There was a quasigovernment organization called the Business Advisory Council that included the leaders of corporate America and members of the executive branch. It did not want members who were not part of the inner circle of American big business. When Hodges insisted that this elite group open its doors to small businesses and that its meetings be open to the press, club members strenuously objected. They did not want outsiders invading what had been a cozy arrangement between themselves and the government, especially after the Eisenhower years when they enjoyed much influence with an overtly probusiness government. A defiant Roger Blough, chief executive officer of United States Steel, informed the president that the corporate chiefs intended to end their relationship with the Business Advisory Council and create their own, private group, the Business Council. Instead of supporting Secretary Hodges, Jack agreed, following the advice of his brother Attorney General Robert Kennedy and Walter Heller, his chairman of the Council of Economic Advisors, to cooperate with Blough's new group. Nevertheless, American business complained that Jack was antibusiness. This tension would be magnified as the Kennedy administration adopted the "new economics."

By the time that Jack assumed the presidency, many economists had adopted the views of the British economist John Maynard Keynes, who claimed that it was advisable for governments to borrow money in order to stimulate economic activity, particularly during economic slowdowns. Referred to as "Keynesians," this school of economic thought was not afraid of governments spending more money than received through taxes, and Jack's administration contained a number of Keynesian economists including Walter Heller who did much to mold Jack's thinking about economic policy. It was through Heller's influence, for example, that Jack came to support a tax cut in the hope that this would spur economic activity.

Yet, Jack faced a challenge in trying to get that tax cut through a Congress reluctant to embrace Keynesian economics. He decided to begin the process of changing minds with an address to the graduating class of Yale University on June 11, 1962. The Yale Commencement Address is one of the most memorable of the Kennedy years. As he worked through many drafts of the speech, Jack was influenced by a conversation he had with French scholar and politician Andre Malraux. The tone of the Malraux-Kennedy discussion was much broader than economic policy. They discussed how "myths" had obscured reality. "Malraux said that in Europe in the nineteenth century the ostensible issue was monarchy vs. the republic, while the real conflict was capitalism vs. the proletariat." In the 1950s and 1960s, Malraux told Jack, the "ostensible" issue remained "capitalism vs. the proletariat."[23] Jack countered that the real issue of contemporary politics "was the management of industrial society, not a problem of ideology, but of administration." According to Arthur Schlesinger Jr., a historian who served on Kennedy's staff, as Jack prepared for the Yale speech "this conversation remained in his mind."[24]

At Yale, Jack announced the end of stereotypes. It was time to allow for new modes of thinking. "The central domestic issues of our time are more subtle and less simple. They relate not to basic clashes of philosophy or ideology but to ways and means of reaching common goals," Jack argued. Although he did not mention tax cuts, or the new economics, he was trying to set the stage for their arrival. Stereotypes, he argued, prevent people from seeing the common interest. It stirs passion—not to accomplish national goals—but to maintain the stereotypes. This he opposed. And he proceeded to bring this into sharp focus in the Yale speech. "For the great enemy of truth is very often not the lie," said Jack, "but the myth." As long as old ideas retain their grip on peoples' minds, the common interest will not be served. "Mythology distracts us everywhere—in government as in business, in politics as in economics, in foreign affairs as in domestic affairs," he pointed out.[25]

Jack focused on three "myths" for his Yale speech, although he made clear there were many more. He discussed the myth of big government, the myth of government spending, and the myth of confidence. "I want," he said, "to talk about all three, and I want to talk about them carefully and dispassionately—and I emphasize that I am concerned here not with political debate but with finding ways to separate false problems from the real ones." Departing from the position he had taken as a congressman in a 1950 speech when he warned against the "ever expanding power of the Federal government," Jack now said that the idea that government was too big was false. "If we leave defense and space expenditures aside, the federal government since the Second World War has expanded less than any other major sector of our national life." Despite this, the myth persisted. The public continued to see "big government" growing bigger. The second myth was the need for a balanced budget. At times, a budget deficit may be good for the nation particularly if inflation remained low. "Obviously, deficits are sometimes dangerous, and so too are surpluses."[26] He pointed out that the current budget deficit was near $10 billion yet inflation was below 1 percent. Finally, he argued that there was not good evidence to suggest that business cycles were linked to the level of confidence in a president's administration. He concluded, reflecting on his conversation with Malraux, "What is at stake in our economic decisions today is not some grand warfare of rival ideologies which will sweep the country with passion." Rather, "the point is that this is basically an administrative or executive problem."[27]

Despite his Yale speech, the proposal to reduce tax rates on income initially failed in the Congress, and inside his administration the president also faced opposition to the plan. Economist John Kenneth Galbraith, a key advisor who also served as the U.S. ambassador to India, favored higher government spending on public works as a way to stimulate economic activity. Galbraith's position was in line with traditional liberal thinking regarding the economy, as public works spending had been used during the Franklin D. Roosevelt administration in programs like the Works Progress Administration, the Public Works Administration, the Civilian Conservation Corps, and the Tennessee Valley Authority. Yet, Jack did not abandon the tax cut proposal. He worked diligently to win passage of the bill. In December 1962, he spoke before the Economic Club of New York where he stressed that a tax cut would be good for the economy struggling through a recession. Both the Business Council and labor organizations ultimately responded favorably. His secretary of the treasury Douglas Dillon, a Republican, worked to win his party's support for the measure. The tax cut bill finally passed the House on September 25, 1963, and was signed into law following Jack's assassination on February 26, 1964, by President Johnson. The tax cut benefited the economy, as growth increased, and the stock market boomed under Lyndon Johnson. Joblessness declined from 5.5 percent in December 1963 to 4.1 percent by December 1965. The growth of the economy moved from 2.5 percent when Jack inherited the presidency from Eisenhower to 6 percent by December 1964. Then, too, inflation held firm and did not increase as a result of the cut in tax rates.

The steel crisis of 1962 also influenced Jack's speech at Yale, because he had a direct confrontation with steel companies over price increases. Due to the numerous steel strikes since the end of World War II, labor unions and management had had a long-standing strained relationship. In addition to the frequent strikes, the cost of steel was an ever-increasing burden for manufacturers, as everything from cars to tanks increased in price as steel became more expensive. As Walter Heller had explained to the president in summer 1961, "Steel bulks so large in the manufacturing sector of the economy that it can upset the applecart all by itself."[28] Accordingly, the Council of Economic Advisors, under Heller's leadership, designed a voluntary "guidepost" program under which both labor and management would hold wage and price increases to productivity gains. In 1962, a contract year, the administration wanted to avoid a labor disruption as well as an increase in prices beyond the guideposts assessed by the Council of Economic Advisors. Secretary of Labor Arthur Goldberg, himself a former labor negotiator, intervened in the negotiations and convinced the labor unions to accept a modest 10 cent an hour increase in benefits and wages. While the steel companies did not actually say they would not increase prices, they gave the labor secretary that impression.

On April 10, 1962, United States Steel chairman Roger Blough met with the president and handed him a piece of paper that had also been released to the press announcing a price increase beyond the guideposts. The president was furious. "You have made a terrible mistake," he told Blough, "you double-crossed me."[29] Jack summoned Labor Secretary Goldberg to the White House. Goldberg, believing that he had failed the president in not ensuring that United States Steel would not raise prices so high, offered his resignation. Jack rejected the offer and called his brother to the White House where they plotted a response. They decided to use the FBI against steel executives personally. FBI agents visited executives at United States Steel, and the administration examined their records to discover any improper activities. During this time, other steel companies followed the example of United States Steel and raised their prices. While Bobby was using the FBI and was beginning a Department of Justice investigation into whether the steel industry had broken any laws, the outraged president prepared to attack United States Steel publically. As he told his staff, "My father always told me that all businessmen were sons of bitches, but I never believed it till now."[30]

At his April 11, 1962, press conference, Jack used words against United States Steel that few presidents have used against American corporations. He began by stating that corporations, like individuals, have obligations to their country. Short-term gains by the corporation must be foregone in order to strengthen the nation. The long-term interest of the corporation was linked to the health of the national economy. Jack stated that the price increase announced by United States Steel was a "wholly unjustifiable and irresponsible defiance of the public interest." Referring to soldiers around the world engaged in the struggle with the Soviet Union, he decried a situation in which corporations could escape their public responsibilities. "When restraint and sacrifice are being asked of every citizen, the American people will find it hard, as I do, to accept a situation in which a tiny handful of steel executives whose pursuit of private power and profit exceeds their sense of public responsibility can show such utter contempt for the interests of 185 million Americans." In a pointed remark, he said, "Some time ago, I asked each American to consider what he would do for his country and I asked the steel companies. In the last 24 hours we had their answer."[31]

Public opinion polls revealed widespread support for the president's approach to the steel crisis, and his approval rating reached 73 percent. Bolstered by these results, Jack instructed the attorney general to determine if steel companies had colluded to fix prices and encouraged Congress to investigate as well. Secretary of Defense McNamara began awarding contracts to steel companies that had not raised prices. The collective effort produced the effect the president sought. All the major steel companies rolled back their price increases. Conservatives and some business leaders, however, were appalled at the president's reaction to the price increases. Arizona senator Barry Goldwater, for example, argued that Jack intended to "socialize the business of the country."[32]

In his early years in the Senate Jack had little interest in or demonstrated much support for the American space program. In the 1960 presidential campaign, he changed his position, repeatedly telling supporters that the United States must surpass the Soviet Union, which had launched *Sputnik,* the first artificial successful satellite, three years earlier. When the National Aeronautics and Space Administration (NASA), in the same year, recommended that the nation place a man on the moon, Jack embraced the idea. After Soviet cosmonaut Yuri Gagarin became the first human in space in an April 1961 orbital flight aboard *Vostok I,* Jack's interest intensified. This triumph gave Nikita Khrushchev the opportunity to claim another victory of the communist system over American capitalism, a view shared by most people around the world. As late as two years later, despite successful Project Mercury space flights including John Glenn's 1962 orbital flight, a global opinion poll revealed that most people continued to believe that the Soviet Union was ahead in space exploration.

On May 25, 1961, only six weeks after the Gagarin flight, Jack offered a lofty goal for his fellow citizens in an appearance before the Congress, calling upon the nation to "commit itself to achieving the goal, before this decade is out, of landing a man on the moon and returning him safely to earth."[33] Estimates of the Project Apollo program ranged as high as $40 billion. Vocal American scientists and many liberals argued that such funding would be better spent on medical research and critical social programs. Public opinion polls revealed that a clear majority of citizens likewise opposed such an expensive project. Undaunted, Jack offered a number of rationales for the space program. In a 1962 press conference, he told reporters, "I do not think the United States can afford to become second in space because I think that space has too many implications militarily, politically, psychologically, and all the rest." He also believed that such an ambitious objective was appropriate for the theme of his administration, the New Frontier, his call for sacrifice for the greater good of the nation. Yet, it was the Cold War context that really drove his willingness to commit so much funding to the project. As he told NASA director James Webb, "Everything we do ought to really be tied in to getting on to the moon ahead of the Russians. Otherwise we shouldn't be spending that kind of money."[34] Ultimately, the president persuaded the nation. By 1965, almost 60 percent responding to a poll endorsed the project.

One other element of the Kennedy administration is worthy of note. While Jack displayed little interest in the various investigations, his brother Bobby led a substantial effort to defeat organized crime in America. In late 1950s, while serving on the McClellan Rackets Committee, Bobby had devoted more than two and one-half years to an investigation, one that focused upon the ties between the powerful International Brotherhood of Teamsters and organized crime. With a staff of more than 100, Bobby participated in hundreds of days of hearings involving more than 1,500 witnesses and more than 20,000 pages of evidence. He saw his work for the committee as a profound education in the power of organized crime. In 1960, Bobby published *The Enemy Within* in which he argued "the gangsters of today work in a highly organized fashion and are far more powerful now than at any time in the history of the country." Because "organized criminals" had so successfully corrupted businesses, unions, and governments, only a concerted national effort to stop them could prevent gangsters from destroying the nation.[35] When his brother appointed him to the post of attorney general, Bobby had an opportunity to attack organized crime. In his testimony before the Senate Judiciary Committee, he stated his intention to "pursue" organized criminals "to the full vigor of the Department of Justice."[36]

Once in office, Bobby targeted more than 1,000 organized crime figures and forced FBI director J. Edgar Hoover to focus less on the internal communist threat and more on organized crime. Hoover complied, dramatically increasing the number of agents investigating gangsters. Bobby also increased the staff at the Justice Department's Organized Crime and Racketeering Section and had the Internal Revenue Service investigate the tax returns of the men he targeted. Las Vegas became a particular focus for the attorney general. Bobby believed that organized

Lieutenant General Leighton I. Davis welcomes the president to Cape Canaveral. In a May 1961, address to a joint session of Congress, Kennedy announced an ambitious initiative to land a man on the moon by the end of the decade. (NASA)

crime figures, using "front" men, had gained control of many of the Las Vegas casinos and had been "skimming" (removing cash from the casino count rooms before recording the daily income from gamblers) money for several years. In the summer of 1961, for example, the Justice Department asked Roger Foley, the attorney general for Nevada, to "deputize sixty-five federal agents" as part of "a federal strike force that was being put together to invade every major casino in Reno and Las Vegas." "Bobby Kennedy," in Governor Grant Sawyer's judgment, "wanted to show the people of the United States that he was the guy to clean up all sin and corruption, and Nevada was a great place to start." Only Sawyer's quick trip to Washington, with Foley in tow, to meet not just with the attorney general, but also with the president, headed off the raid.[37] Among the many gangsters Bobby investigated, Carlos Marcello, the head of organized crime activity in New Orleans, became a key target for the attorney general. In 1961, Bobby used the Immigration and Naturalization Service to deport Marcello to Guatemala. The results of this collective effort were dramatic. In 1960, the Justice Department had indicted only 9 gangsters, but in 1963 that figure reached 615.

By the fall of 1963, Jack Kennedy had scored a number of domestic policy victories fulfilling several campaign pledges. Millions of workers benefited from a slightly higher minimum wage, the unemployed in several economically depressed areas of the country had access to job training, and all taxpayers were enjoying the benefits of a tax cut. Further, he had laid the foundations for the passage of a comprehensive civil rights bill as well as a bill for the public financing of health insurance for the elderly. A trip to Dallas in November 1963 prevented him from seeing the fruition of the work he had begun in the first thousand days of his administration.

NOTES

1. Carl M. Brauer, *John F. Kennedy and the Second Reconstruction* (New York: Columbia University Press, 1977), p. 79.

2. John F. Kennedy, *John Fitzgerald Kennedy: A Compilation of Statements and Speeches Made during His Service in the United States Senate*

and House of Representatives (Washington, DC: Government Printing Office, 1964), p. 541.

3. John F. Kennedy, *John Fitzgerald Kennedy*, p. 539.

4. John F. Kennedy, *Freedom of Communications, Part One: The Speeches, Remarks, Press Conferences and Statements of Senator John F. Kennedy, August 1 through November 7, 1960* (Washington, DC: Government Printing Office, 1961), pp. 550 and 1112.

5. Allan Nevins, ed., *The Burden and the Glory: The Hopes and Purposes of President Kennedy's Second and Third Years in Office as Revealed in His Public Statements and Addresses* (New York: Harper & Row, 1964), pp. 167–168.

6. Nevins, *Burden and the Glory*, p. 169.

7. Robert Dallek, *An Unfinished Life: John F. Kennedy, 1917–1963* (New York: Back Bay Books, 2003), p. 515.

8. James N. Giglio, *The Presidency of John F. Kennedy*, 2nd ed. (Lawrence: University Press of Kansas, 2006), p. 195.

9. Harris Wofford, *Of Kennedys and Kings: Making Sense of the Sixties* (New York: Farrar, Straus & Giroux, 1980), p. 173.

10. Richard Reeves, *President Kennedy: Profile of Power* (New York: Touchstone, 1993), p. 488.

11. Dallek, *An Unfinished Life*, p. 600.

12. Reeves, *President Kennedy*, pp. 488 and 489.

13. Nevins, *Burden and the Glory*, p. 181.

14. Nevins, *Burden and the Glory*, p. 183.

15. Nevins, *Burden and the Glory*, p. 182.

16. Nevins, *Burden and the Glory*, p. 183.

17. Michael O'Brien, *John Kennedy: A Biography* (New York: Thomas Dunne Books, 2005), pp. 839 and 840.

18. Irving Bernstein, *Promises Kept: John F. Kennedy's New Frontier* (New York: Oxford University Press, 1991), p. 103.

19. Theodore C. Sorensen, *Kennedy* (New York: Harper and Row, 1965), p. 496.

20. Dallek, *An Unfinished Life*, p. 642.

21. Bernstein, *Promises Kept*, p. 249.

22. Bernstein, *Promises Kept*, p. 256.

23. Bernstein, *Promises Kept*, p. 146.

24. Arthur M. Schlesinger Jr., *A Thousand Days: John F. Kennedy in the White House* (Boston: Houghton Mifflin, 1965), p. 644.

25. *Public Papers of the Presidents of the United States: John F. Kennedy, 1962* (Washington, DC: Government Printing Office, 1963), pp. 470–471.

26. *Public Papers* (1963), pp. 471–472.

27. Reeves, *President Kennedy*, p. 321.

28. Reeves, *President Kennedy*, p. 294.

29. Reeves, *President Kennedy*, p. 296.

30. Giglio, *Presidency of John F. Kennedy*, p. 132.

31. *Public Papers* (1963), pp. 315–317.

32. Dallek, *An Unfinished Life*, p. 488.

33. Giglio, *Presidency of John F. Kennedy*, p. 153.

34. Dallek, *An Unfinished Life*, pp. 651 and 652.

35. Robert F. Kennedy, *The Enemy Within* (New York: Harper & Row, 1960), pp. 240 and 265.

36. "Excerpts from the Testimony of Robert Kennedy before Senate Panel," *New York Times*, January 14, 1961, p. 8.

37. *Hang Tough! Grant Sawyer: An Activist in the Governor's Mansion* (Reno: University of Nevada Oral History Program, 1993), pp. 89–91

Chapter 8

EXPLAINING THE
ASSASSINATION

When Jack traveled to Dallas, Texas, in late November 1963, he encountered a city with a reputation for right-wing extremism. In 1960
residents had spit on Lady Bird Johnson, and only a month before the
president's visit, a crowd jeered United Nations Ambassador Adlai
Stevenson; one woman struck him on the head with an anti-UN sign.
The day before the president's arrival someone distributed about 5,000
leaflets claiming Kennedy was "Wanted for Treason." Some on the president's staff had urged him not to make the trip. When Jack arrived in
Dallas for his fateful visit, he was greeted by a full-page ad in the *Dallas
Morning News* accusing him and his brother of being weak on communism. "We're heading into nut country today," he muttered to Jackie as
he read the paper. He added, "if somebody wants to shoot me from a
window with a rifle, nobody can stop it."[1] To prevent such a tragedy,
more than 300 Dallas policemen, 40 state policemen, and more than a
dozen county deputy sheriffs were assigned to protect the president.

Complicating matters, there were tensions within the Texas Democratic Party between factions led by conservative governor John Connally and liberal senator John Yarborough. Jack had barely won the
state in 1960 with Lyndon Johnson on the ticket, so he hoped this trip

would reassure his supporters during stops in San Antonio, Houston, and Fort Worth before reaching Dallas. To illustrate the unity of the Democratic Party in Texas, the president would ride in the motorcade with Governor Connally, and Vice President Johnson would ride with Senator Yarborough.

Despite the initial concerns, Jack and Jackie received a cordial welcome from a crowd of nearly 2,000 at the airport. As they traveled through downtown Dallas on November 22, 1963, large crowds of about 150,000 people greeted them warmly along the route. Jack even stopped the motorcade along the parade route to greet some nuns who had come to see the president. The weather was beautiful, and everything seemed to be going well as the motorcade left the downtown area. Unknown to the Secret Service, Lee Harvey Oswald had taken a position on the sixth floor of the Texas Schoolbook Depository building.

A frustrated and angry 24-year-old man, Lee Harvey Oswald had become a Marxist in his mid-teens, joined the Marines at 17, and, after studying Russian, emigrated to the Soviet Union in 1959. While there,

The Kennedy motorcade in Dallas shortly before President Kennedy was assassinated, on November 22, 1963. Texas governor John Connally and his wife, Nellie, are in the front seat, with President and Mrs. Kennedy seated in back. (Library of Congress)

he married Marina Pruskova. Oswald brought his wife with him when he returned to the United States in 1962. Settling in the Dallas area, he moved from one low-paying job to another. In early 1963, Oswald purchased a revolver and a rifle. In the spring of that year he moved to his hometown of New Orleans looking for steady employment. Surviving largely on unemployment checks, he began planning a move to Cuba with the intention of returning to the USSR. While in New Orleans, he joined the Fair Play for Cuba Committee, a pro-Castro group. (He was the only member of the New Orleans branch.) He handed out leaflets supporting Cuba and even engaged in a radio debate defending the Castro regime. In September, Oswald traveled by bus to Mexico City, hoping to obtain a travel visa to Cuba, but neither the Cuban nor the Russian embassy would issue him one. He returned to Dallas in early October and obtained a job at the Texas School Depository building.

Ahead of the president's motorcade in Dealey Plaza was the "grassy knoll," an open area that some in the crowd would identify as the source of the shots. As the motorcade entered this area, Texas first lady Nellie Connally turned and said to Jack, "Mr. President, they can't make you believe now that there are not some in Dallas who love you and appreciate you, can they?"[2] Seconds later, a bullet hit Jack in the back of the neck and exited through his throat. The Secret Service agent riding in the front seat of the presidential limousine thought Jack said, "My God, I'm hit." The bullet then struck Governor Connally, and he cried out, "They're going to kill us all." Jack grabbed his neck and throat, and Jackie moved to help her husband. As she did so, the president's head exploded, with blood and brain matter going everywhere. Jackie screamed, "They've killed my husband! They've shot his head off!"[3] She tried to get out of the car crawling onto the trunk, but was saved by Secret Service agent Clint Hill who leaped onto the car and pushed Jackie back into the seat. Once the driver realized what had happened, he proceeded rapidly to Parkland Memorial Hospital. Oswald left the Texas Schoolbook Depository building and 45 minutes later, he shot and killed Dallas police officer J. D. Tippet. Oswald took refuge in a movie theater where police took him into custody.

As the presidential motorcade arrived at Parkland Hospital, Jackie was cradling her husband's head in her lap, and she was reluctant to allow hospital staff to take him from her. Once the president was taken into a trauma room, she remained close by and at one point knelt and prayed. Doctors began efforts to resuscitate Jack, and, focused on that, did not notice the extent of the president's head wound. They struggled to maintain a steady heart rhythm. However, once they realized the extent of his head wound, the doctors stopped the efforts to save the president. Two Roman Catholic priests were summoned to give the Last Rites of the Catholic Church. Within an hour of the assassination, the press was informed of the president's death.

Controversy reigned at Parkland Hospital after Kennedy's death. Under Texas law, autopsies of homicide victims had to be performed in Texas. Dr. Earl Rose, the Dallas County medical examiner, and Theron Ward, a justice of the peace, insisted on following Texas law, much to the anger of the president's aides and the Secret Service detail. Literally, a struggle over possession of the body ensued at the hospital, with Secret Service agents forcing their way out of the hospital. The incident would later suggest to conspiracy theorists that there had been a government cover-up of the assassination.

On the morning of November 24, Dallas detectives took Lee Harvey Oswald from his jail cell in the municipal building to transfer him to the county jail about a mile away. As two detectives held their suspect in the basement of the municipal building, a man named Jack Ruby stepped forward and shot Oswald in the side. Ruby, a frequent visitor to the municipal building, later claimed to be distraught over the president's death and had decided to take revenge. The shooting was particularly shocking to an already-stunned public because it took place during live television coverage.

In light of the extraordinary events of the previous three days, shortly after Kennedy's funeral on November 25, the Johnson White House announced that the Justice Department would "conduct a prompt and thorough investigation of all the circumstances surrounding the brutal assassination of President Kennedy and the murder of his alleged assassin."[4] Four days later, President Johnson also named an independent seven-man commission to investigate the assassination. Senators Richard B. Russell and John S. Cooper, Representatives Hale Boggs and Gerald R. Ford, former CIA director Allen W. Dulles, and John J. McCloy, former president of the World Bank, joined Chief Justice Earl

Warren to pursue the president's directive "to evaluate all available information concerning the subject of the inquiry."[5] The Warren Commission began its investigation the following week and delivered an
888-page report with 26 supplementary volumes to President Johnson
on September 24, 1964. Drawing upon more than 26,000 interviews
conducted by the FBI and Secret Service, as well as testimony from
94 witnesses who appeared before the commission staff as well as forensic and ballistic evidence, the seven-man panel concluded that Lee
Harvey Oswald had acted alone in murdering the president. Because
of the rapid growth of public skepticism about the Warren Commission's findings over the following decade, the House of Representatives
appointed another select committee in September 1976 to take a second official look at the evidence. The committee delivered its report
in early 1979, and while concluding that Lee Harvey Oswald did fire
three shots at Kennedy, it did stipulate that there was "a high probabil-
ity" that two gunmen fired at the president. The committee drew this
conclusion largely on acoustic evidence of a recording from a police
motorcycle microphone (evidence discredited three years later) indicating a fourth gunshot. Indeed, the committee reported, "President John F.
Kennedy was probably assassinated as result of a conspiracy." However, the committee was unable to identify who else may have been
involved, absolving the Soviet and Cuban governments, anti-Castro
Cubans, organized crime, the Secret Service, the FBI, and the CIA.[6] In
1992, Congress passed legislation creating an Assassination Records
Review Board, an independent agency, to identify and release documents related to Kennedy's assassination. Six years later, the board
made its final report, releasing 90,000 documents with a promise of the
release of all the documents by 2017. However, according to the *New
York Times*, the release revealed "no second gunman, no assassin skulk-
ing on the grassy knoll, no vast conspiracy."[7]

The Assassination Records Review Board nonetheless acknowledged that the federal government had not handled the investigation
into the Kennedy assassination well: "the suspicions created by Government secrecy eroded confidence in the truthfulness of Federal agen-
cies in general and damaged their credibility."[8] Indeed, from the day of
the assassination most Americans have refused to believe the official
explanation for President Kennedy's assassination. A public opinion

poll taken within a week of the president's funeral revealed that only 24 percent believed that Oswald acted alone. Consistently from that date, polls show that about 75 percent believe that Kennedy died as a result of a conspiracy. It is also true that some close to the president likewise worried that a conspiracy was involved. On the day of the assassination, Robert Kennedy consulted his contacts inside and outside the government, wanting to know if they had evidence of any involvement of the CIA, anti-Castro Cubans, or the Mafia in his brother's death. President Johnson acknowledged to a newsman in 1964 that he believed that the Cuban government may have been involved because of CIA efforts to eliminate Castro.

These doubts have been fueled by a steady stream of conspiracy advocates. Starting with Thomas Buchanan's *Who Killed Kennedy?* (1964) and Mark Lane's *Rush to Judgment* (1966), there have been more than 2,000 books and articles that have spun an amazing number of conspiracy theories, an effort supplemented by the release of dozens of movies, documentaries, and television specials. Now, the field is dominated by a seemingly endless number of Internet blogs that claim a bewildering range of conspirators and co-conspirators: Lyndon Johnson, Nikita Khrushchev, far-right wealthy Texans, international drug lords, the John Birch Society, George H. W. Bush, and the Secret Service are just a few of the alleged conspirators.

While there seems to be no end to the number of conspiracy theories, five have attracted the most attention because in the judgment of the conspiracy theorists, these conspirators had the best motives for eliminating the president: organized crime figures, the Cuban government, anti-Castro Cubans, the CIA and FBI, and the military-industrial complex. Conspiracy theorists ascribe the following motives to these groups. Mobsters like Sam Giancana felt betrayed by the Kennedy administration for its vigorous prosecution of organized crime after they had helped turn out the vote for Kennedy in 1960 and had worked with his CIA in attempts to assassinate Fidel Castro. Carlos Marcello, the kingpin of organized crime in New Orleans, had allegedly vowed vengeance on the president because his Justice Department had deported Marcello in 1961. Fidel Castro, knowing about the CIA-backed efforts to kill him, had allegedly claimed in September 1963 that U.S. officials would be targeted if the assassination attempts on him persisted. Anti-

Castro Cuban exiles in the United States, and Americans like Clay Shaw and David Ferrie who supported them, hated Kennedy because he had failed to fully back the Bay of Pigs assault in 1961. The CIA likewise felt betrayed by Kennedy in that episode and also feared that the president was prepared to weaken their agency; J. Edgar Hoover feared that Kennedy and his brother wanted to remove him as director of the FBI. Finally, defense contractors worried that Kennedy was moving toward détente with the Soviet Union and that he intended to minimize the U.S. role in Vietnam, moves that would threaten their profits and diminish their influence with the federal government. For conspiracy advocates, these theories made for compelling stories, but evidence to support the claims is slight, circumstantial, or simply nonexistent.

Oliver Stone is the most influential conspiracy theorist. Movie critics hailed his 1991 film *JFK* as a riveting political thriller with a gallery of Hollywood luminaries including Kevin Costner, Tommy Lee Jones, Donald Sutherland, Walther Matthau, Jack Lemmon, Gary Oldman, Ed Asner, and Joe Pesci. The film portrays an investigation from 1967 to 1969 led by New Orleans district attorney Jim Garrison that ended with an indictment and trial of New Orleans businessman Clay Shaw for taking part in a conspiracy to assassinate the president. After less than an hour of deliberations, the jury acquitted Shaw. Stone used Garrison as a protagonist for many conspiracy advocates. Employing a mysterious character known as Mr. X and Garrison's closing statement in the Shaw trial, Stone drew a remarkable range of people into the conspiracy—the CIA, defense contractors, Big Oil, the Dallas police force, the Secret Service, Lyndon Johnson, the FBI, and the heads of all the military services. This conspiracy had no face. Yet, it targeted a president intent upon withdrawing American troops from Vietnam. It was an invisible government, and it successfully executed a coup d'état using Lee Harvey Oswald as a "patsy." As *Time* magazine explained, "So, you want to know who killed the President and connived in the cover-up? High officials in the CIA, the FBI, the Dallas constabulary, all three armed services, Big Business and the White House. Everybody done it—everybody but Lee Harvey Oswald."[9]

Amidst all these conspiracy theories, three works have demonstrated clearly that Lee Harvey Oswald was John Kennedy's assassin. In 1986 the Showtime cable network broadcast a program entitled "On Trial: Lee Harvey Oswald." This mock trial featured a real judge, 12 Dallas jurors, and 24 witnesses, including people who had witnessed the assassination, pathologists, and ballistics experts who appeared voluntarily. The film of the assassination taken by Abraham Zapruder was one of the many exhibits used in the program. Vincent Bugliosi, who had successfully prosecuted serial killer Charles Manson, presented the government's case, and famed defense attorney Gerry Spence represented Oswald. The five-hour jury trial ended in Oswald's conviction.

Two books, *Case Closed: Lee Harvey Oswald and the Assassination of JFK* (1993) by Gerald Posner and *Reclaiming History: The Assassination of President John F. Kennedy* (2007) by the same Vincent Bugliosi who appeared on the Showtime docu-trial, emphatically endorsed the findings of the Warren Commission that Oswald had acted alone. Posner's 607-page tome pales in comparison to the mammoth 2,792-page (1,128 pages of footnotes are on a CD-ROM) book produced by Bugliosi. The two authors systematically confront and dismantle the leading conspiracy theories by thoroughly examining the key forensic and ballistic evidence and reviewing witness testimony. Arguments that the FBI, CIA, KGB, military-industrial complex, organized crime, or Fidel Castro, among many others, were involved in a conspiracy are left in tatters by Posner and Bugliosi.

Despite the herculean efforts of these two authors, most Americans remain convinced that Oswald could not have acted alone. Some are fascinated by the puzzle and the intrigue. Many cannot overcome their distrust of the government, a skepticism fueled by disclosures of CIA and FBI wrongdoing and the Watergate scandal. Others refuse to accept the possibility that a delusional loner could eliminate the most powerful man in the world. In other words, they seek a sense of proportion. William Manchester, in *Death of a President*, explained, "If you put the murdered President of the United States on one side of a scale and that wretched waif Oswald on the other side, it doesn't balance. You want to add something weightier to Oswald. . . . A conspiracy would, of course, do nicely." Similarly, Kennedy confidant Theodore Sorensen wrote, 45 years after the assassination, "many people all over the world, including me, would feel somewhat better knowing, with a certainty, even now, that John F. Kennedy was killed by ideological adversaries, and thus died a martyr for a cause, and not simply in a senseless killing at the hands of a crazed lucky sharpshooter."[10]

NOTES

1. Robert Dallek, *An Unfinished Life: John F. Kennedy, 1917–1963* (New York: Back Bay Books, 2003), p. 693.

2. Vincent Bugliosi, *Reclaiming History: The Assassination of President John F. Kennedy* (New York: W. W. Norton, 2007), p. 37.

3. Gerald Blaine, with Lisa McCubbin, *The Kennedy Detail: JFK's Secret Service Agents Break Their Silence* (New York: Gallery Books, 2010), pp. 214 and 216.

4. Cabell Phillips, "Johnson Pledges Facts in Killings," *New York Times,* November 26, 1963, p. 15.

5. John D. Morris, "Johnson Names a 7-Man Panel to Investigate Assassination," *New York Times,* November 30, 1963, p. 1.

6. *Final Report of the Select Committee on Assassinations,* U.S. House of Representatives, 95th Congress, 2nd Session (Washington, DC: Government Printing Office, 1979), p. 3.

7. Tim Weiner, "A Blast at Secrecy in Kennedy Killing," *New York Times,* September 29, 1998, p. A17.

8. Weiner, "Blast," p. A17.

9. Richard Corliss, "Who Killed J.F.K.?" *Time,* December 23, 1991, p. 67.

10. Quoted in Christopher Lehmann-Haupt, "Kennedy Assassination Answers," *New York Times,* September 9, 1993, p. C18 and Theodore C. Sorensen, *Counselor: A Life at the Edge of History* (New York: HarperCollins, 2008), p. 374.

Chapter 9

CAMELOT

The nation came to a standstill for the funeral of John F. Kennedy, the first president to die from an assassin's bullet since William McKinley in 1901. Leaders from around the world attended the state event including Charles de Gaulle of France, Ludwig Erhard of West Germany, Emperor Haile Selasie of Ethiopia, and Prince Philip, husband of Elizabeth II of Great Britain. The funeral of John Kennedy was modeled after that of Abraham Lincoln in 1865. As with the 16th president's funeral, after a private viewing in the East Room of the White House, the president's body lay in state in the Capitol Rotunda on a catafalque that had been used in Lincoln's funeral. More than a quarter of a million mourners filed past the president's casket. On November 25, a riderless horse trailed behind the caisson taking the president's body, as in Lincoln's funeral, from the Capitol to St. Matthew's Roman Catholic Cathedral for a requiem mass. During the funeral march, which included the First Lady and the Kennedy brothers Robert and Edward, from the cathedral to Arlington National Cemetery, the mourners heard muffled drums again as with Lincoln's funeral. The nation and the world saw the dead president's widow leading not only her immediate family in grieving, but the nation. There were images like a young John Fitzgerald Kennedy Jr.

saluting his father's casket that remain seared into the memory of Americans of that generation. Jacqueline Kennedy's poise, control, and dignity on display on television screens impressed people around the world.

Theodore H. White, journalist and author of *The Making of the President* (1960), wrote movingly of those remarkable days in November:

> There was in the drama of four days all things to bind all men: a hero, slain; a villain; a sorrowing wife; a stricken mother and family; and two enchanting children. So broad was the emotional span, embracing every member of every family from child to grandparent, that it made the grief of the Kennedys a common grief.[1]

John F. Kennedy Jr., age three, salutes his father's casket in Washington, DC, on November 25, 1963. With Jacqueline Kennedy (center) and her daughter, Caroline, are Senator Edward M. Kennedy, left, and Attorney General Robert F. Kennedy. (AP Photo)

John F. Kennedy had been America's first television president, and his death, like his time as the nation's chief executive, was made for television. It all seemed so improbable. This young man, with a young family, leading a young and vigorous America, was suddenly gone. Although the new president, Lyndon Johnson, had the support of the American people, he was not John Kennedy. He was not charismatic, young, well-spoken, and he certainly was not made for television. A Southern accent, one ill-suited for television or indeed for radio, replaced the Boston accent of the dead president. Some would say later that the America of innocence and optimism died in Dallas in 1963, and in Washington, at Jack's funeral. In one sense that may be true, as much unhappiness and suffering awaited the new president and the nation for the rest of the decade.

In the weeks following her husband's death, Jacqueline Kennedy tried to set the tone for the writing of the history of her husband's administration. She was particularly intent that academic historians, whom she called bitter old men, not be allowed to, in her view, distort and demean the record of her husband's administration. She invited Theodore White to her home only a week after the president's assassination. He was preparing an article for a special issue of *Life* magazine. At one point in the interview she related to White that the president enjoyed listening to records and his favorite was the popular Broadway musical *Camelot*. He particularly enjoyed these lines from the final number of the play: "Don't let it be forgot, that once there was a spot, for one brief shining moment that was known as Camelot." Jack's widow emphasized to White, "There'll be great Presidents again—and the Johnsons are wonderful, they've been wonderful to me—but there'll never be another Camelot again."[2] Writers of the Camelot genre described a man who was, quite frankly, more than he had ever been as president. They focused upon the cultivated, charming intellect so gifted at witty repartee with journalists at more than 60 press conferences and the president, when hosting several Nobel Prize winners, who could say, "This is the most extraordinary collection of talent, of human knowledge, that has ever been gathered together at the White House, with the possible exception of when Thomas Jefferson dined here alone."[3] He and Jackie were the attractive couple known for more than 60 state dinners at the White House, occasions that usually included performances by Broadway stars, the American Shakespeare Festival Theater, and famed cellist Pablo Casals. This view of the Kennedys endured for some time, a larger-than-life, glamorous time at the White House.

In this movement to enshrine the legacy of Kennedy as a truly great leader, many writers forgot to mention the stalled legislative programs in Congress, or the mistakes Jack had made in foreign policy. At this date, no one dared to probe into President Kennedy's private life and reveal to the public the tawdry behavior he exhibited throughout his life. In 1963, few were thinking of Vietnam, and, in any case, the blame for the debacle would rest with President Johnson.

So strong was the public's admiration for the dead president that there was a move to make Robert F. Kennedy the vice presidential running mate for Lyndon Johnson in 1964. Bobby Kennedy actively encouraged this effort on his behalf. Some of Jack's advisors, who detested Johnson, and who could not bring themselves to accept him as the new president, were determined to force Johnson to add Bobby to the 1964 ticket. Yet, the truth is that Johnson and Bobby hated each other and would have been wholly incompatible as president and vice president. Bobby had treated Johnson badly following his brother's assassination, even rushing past the 6-foot, 4-inch Texan on Air Force One as it landed at Andrews Air Force Base carrying his brother's body. He did not even acknowledge the new president, and this hurt Johnson deeply. Be that as it may, as the time for the Democratic National Convention in 1964 approached, the Kennedy team, as it had for Jack, rallied on behalf of Bobby to make him the vice presidential nominee of the Democratic Party. It did not matter that Bobby was only 38, had never been elected to an office, and had been made attorney general simply because he was Jack's brother. In the end, Johnson resisted these efforts to attach a Kennedy annex to the Johnson presidency. Yet, Bobby ran for Senate in New York and won in 1964, and in 1968 he challenged President Johnson for renomination. It was Johnson's greatest nightmare that he would be remembered as the mistake between two Kennedy presidents. Tragically, Bobby's quest to regain what his brother had lost to an assassin's bullet in 1963 was itself ended by an assassin's bullet in 1968. Many now began to speak of the Kennedy tragedy: Joe Jr. killed in action in 1944, Kick dead in a plane crash in 1948, Jack felled by an assassin's bullet in 1963, and then Bobby. Tragically still, more sorrow lay ahead for the Kennedy family. In 1999, John F. Kennedy Jr. and his wife died when their private plane was lost off the coast of New England.

In the end, the Camelot image, though tarnished, still resonates with most Americans. Although Kennedy has slipped in the rankings of presidents by historians and political scientists, he remains the most popular among Americans. A poll by U.S. News and World Report in 2009, for example, had Kennedy topping all other presidents with a 70 percent approval rating.[4] For most Americans, then, the image has become the reality. It is a realization of the hope expressed in 1965 by historian Arthur Schlesinger Jr., a Kennedy loyalist. Even though it is nearly half a century after the assassination, many Americans have concluded along with Schlesinger, "the energies," Kennedy "released, the standards he set, the purposes he inspired, the goals he established would guide the land he loved for years to come."[5]

NOTES

1. Quoted in James Piereson, Camelot and the Cultural Revolution: How the Assassination of John F. Kennedy Shattered American Liberalism (New York: Encounter Books, 2009), p. 100.

2. Theodore H. White, "An Epilogue," Life, December 6, 1963, p. 158.

3. Michael O'Brien, Rethinking Kennedy: An Interpretive Biography (Chicago: Ivan R. Dee, 2009), p. 194.

4. "Top 5 Most Popular Presidents: Kennedy, Ike, Bush 41, Clinton, Johnson," U.S. News and World Report, January 5, 2009, http//www. usnews.com/opinion/articles/2009/01/05/top-5-most-popular (accessed June 17, 2010).

5. Arthur M. Schlesinger Jr., A Thousand Days: John F. Kennedy in the White House (Boston: Houghton Mifflin, 1965), p. 1031.

Appendix

A SELECTION OF SPEECHES BY PRESIDENT JOHN F. KENNEDY

DOCUMENT: INAUGURAL ADDRESS

Date: January 20, 1961

Significance: John F. Kennedy's Inaugural Address is one of the best of the 20th century, delivered with eloquence and a call for sacrifice as Kennedy became the first president born in the 20th century.

Source: *Public Papers of the Presidents of the United States: John F. Kennedy* (Washington, DC: Government Printing Office, 1962), pp. 1–3.

Vice President Johnson, Mr. Speaker, Mr. Chief Justice, President Eisenhower, Vice President Nixon, President Truman, Reverend Clergy, fellow citizens:

We observe today not a victory of party but a celebration of freedom—symbolizing an end as well as a beginning—signifying renewal as well as change. For I have sworn before you and Almighty God the same solemn oath our forbears prescribed nearly a century and three-quarters ago.

The world is very different now. For man holds in his mortal hands the power to abolish all forms of human poverty and all forms of human life. And yet the same revolutionary beliefs for which our forebears fought are still at issue around the globe—the belief that the rights of man come not from the generosity of the state but from the hand of God.

We dare not forget today that we are the heirs of that first revolution. Let the word go forth from this time and place, to friend and foe alike, that the torch has been passed to a new generation of Americans—born in this century, tempered by war, disciplined by a hard and bitter peace, proud of our ancient heritage—and unwilling to witness or permit the slow undoing of those human rights to which this nation has always been committed, and to which we are committed today at home and around the world.

Let every nation know, whether it wishes us well or ill, that we shall pay any price, bear any burden, meet any hardship, support any friend, oppose any foe to assure the survival and the success of liberty.

This much we pledge—and more.

To those old allies whose cultural and spiritual origins we share, we pledge the loyalty of faithful friends. United there is little we cannot do in a host of cooperative ventures. Divided there is little we can do—for we dare not meet a powerful challenge at odds and split asunder.

To those new states whom we welcome to the ranks of the free, we pledge our word that one form of colonial control shall not have passed away merely to be replaced by a far more iron tyranny. We shall not always expect to find them supporting our view. But we shall always hope to find them strongly supporting their own freedom—and to remember that, in the past, those who foolishly sought power by riding the back of the tiger ended up inside.

To those people in the huts and villages of half the globe struggling to break the bonds of mass misery, we pledge our best efforts to help them help themselves, for whatever period is required—not because the communists may be doing it, not because we seek their votes, but because it is right. If a free society cannot help the many who are poor, it cannot save the few who are rich.

To our sister republics south of our border, we offer a special pledge—to convert our good words into good deeds—in a new alliance for progress—to assist free men and free governments in casting off the chains of poverty. But this peaceful revolution of hope cannot become the prey of hostile powers. Let all our neighbors know that we shall join with them to oppose aggression or subversion anywhere in the Americas. And let every other power know that this Hemisphere intends to remain the master of its own house.

To that world assembly of sovereign states, the United Nations, our last best hope in an age where the instruments of war have far outpaced the instruments of peace, we renew our pledge of support—to prevent it from becoming merely a forum for invective—to strengthen its shield of the new and the weak—and to enlarge the area in which its writ may run.

Finally, to those nations who would make themselves our adversary, we offer not a pledge but a request: that both sides begin anew the quest for peace, before the dark powers of destruction unleashed by science engulf all humanity in planned or accidental self-destruction.

We dare not tempt them with weakness. For only when our arms are sufficient beyond doubt can we be certain beyond doubt that they will never be employed.

But neither can two great and powerful groups of nations take comfort from our present course—both sides overburdened by the cost of modern weapons, both rightly alarmed by the steady spread of the deadly atom, yet both racing to alter that uncertain balance of terror that stays the hand of mankind's final war.

So let us begin anew—remembering on both sides that civility is not a sign of weakness, and sincerity is always subject to proof. Let us never negotiate out of fear. But let us never fear to negotiate.

Let both sides explore what problems unite us instead of belaboring those problems which divide us.

Let both sides, for the first time, formulate serious and precise proposals for the inspection and control of arms—and bring the absolute power to destroy other nations under the absolute control of all nations.

Let both sides seek to invoke the wonders of science instead of its terrors. Together let us explore the stars, conquer the deserts, eradicate disease, tap the ocean depths and encourage the arts and commerce.

Let both sides unite to heed in all corners of the earth the command of Isaiah—to "undo the heavy burdens . . . (and) let the oppressed go free."

And if a beachhead of cooperation may push back the jungle of suspicion, let both sides join in creating a new endeavor, not a new balance of power, but a new world of law, where the strong are just and the weak secure and the peace preserved.

All this will not be finished in the first one hundred days. Nor will it be finished in the first one thousand days, nor in the life of this Administration, nor even perhaps in our lifetime on this planet. But let us begin.

In your hands, my fellow citizens, more than mine, will rest the final success or failure of our course. Since this country was founded, each generation of Americans has been summoned to give testimony to its national loyalty. The graves of young Americans who answered the call to service surround the globe.

Now the trumpet summons us again—not as a call to bear arms, though arms we need—not as a call to battle, though embattled we are—but a call to bear the burden of a long twilight struggle, year in and year out, "rejoicing in hope, patient in tribulation"—a struggle against the common enemies of man: tyranny, poverty, disease and war itself.

Can we forge against these enemies a grand and global alliance, North and South, East and West, that can assure a more fruitful life for all mankind? Will you join in that historic effort?

In the long history of the world, only a few generations have been granted the role of defending freedom in its hour of maximum danger. I do not shrink from this responsibility—I welcome it. I do not believe that any of us would exchange places with any other people or any other generation. The energy, the faith, the devotion which we bring to this endeavor will light our country and all who serve it—and the glow from that fire can truly light the world.

And so, my fellow Americans: ask not what your country can do for you—ask what you can do for your country.

My fellow citizens of the world: ask not what America will do for you, but what together we can do for the freedom of man.

Finally, whether you are citizens of America or citizens of the world, ask of us here the same high standards of strength and sacrifice which we ask of you. With a good conscience our only sure reward, with history the final judge of our deeds, let us go forth to lead the land we love, asking His blessing and His help, but knowing that here on earth God's work must truly be our own.

DOCUMENT: RADIO AND TELEVISION REPORT TO THE AMERICAN PEOPLE ON THE SOVIET ARMS BUILDUP IN CUBA

Date: October 22, 1962

Significance: In this speech, President Kennedy informs the nation of the dangerous situation in Cuba and of the grave consequences it might pose to world peace. Kennedy informs the nation that a nuclear war between the two superpowers is a possibility.

Source: John F. Kennedy Presidential Library and Museum.

Good evening my fellow citizens:

This Government, as promised, has maintained the closest surveillance of the Soviet Military buildup on the island of Cuba. Within the past week, unmistakable evidence has established the fact that a series of offensive missile sites is now in preparation on that imprisoned island. The purpose of these bases can be none other than to provide a nuclear strike capability against the Western Hemisphere.

Upon receiving the first preliminary hard information of this nature last Tuesday morning at 9 A.M., I directed that our surveillance be stepped up. And having now confirmed and completed our evaluation of the evidence and our decision on a course of action, this Government feels obliged to report this new crisis to you in fullest detail.

The characteristics of these new missile sites indicate two distinct types of installations. Several of them include medium range ballistic missiles capable of carrying a nuclear warhead for a distance of more than 1,000 nautical miles. Each of these missiles, in short, is capable of striking Washington, D.C., the Panama Canal, Cape Canaveral, Mexico City, or any other city in the southeastern part of the United States, in Central America, or in the Caribbean area.

Additional sites not yet completed appear to be designed for intermediate range ballistic missiles—capable of traveling more than twice as far—and thus capable of striking most of the major cities in the Western Hemisphere, ranging as far north as Hudson Bay, Canada, and as far south as Lima, Peru. In addition, jet bombers, capable of carrying nuclear weapons, are now being uncrated and assembled in Cuba, while the necessary air bases are being prepared.

This urgent transformation of Cuba into an important strategic base—by the presence of these large, long range, and clearly offensive weapons of sudden mass destruction—constitutes an explicit threat to the peace and security of all the Americas, in flagrant and deliberate defiance of the Rio Pact of 1947, the traditions of this Nation and hemisphere, the joint resolution of the 87th Congress, the Charter of the United Nations, and my own public warnings to the Soviets on September 4 and 13. This action also contradicts the repeated assurances of Soviet spokesmen, both publicly and privately delivered, that the arms buildup in Cuba would retain its original defensive character, and that the Soviet Union had no need or desire to station strategic missiles on the territory of any other nation.

The size of this undertaking makes clear that it has been planned for some months. Yet only last month, after I had made clear the distinction between any introduction of ground-to-ground missiles and the existence of defensive antiaircraft missiles, the Soviet Government publicly stated on September 11, and I quote, "the armaments and military equipment sent to Cuba are designed exclusively for defensive purposes," that, and I quote the Soviet Government, "there is no need for the Soviet Government to shift its weapons . . . for a retaliatory blow to any other country, for instance Cuba," and that, and I quote their government, "the Soviet Union has so powerful rockets to carry these nuclear warheads that there is no need to search for sites for them beyond the boundaries of the Soviet Union." That statement was false.

Only last Thursday, as evidence of this rapid offensive buildup was already in my hand, Soviet Foreign Minister Gromyko told me in my office that he was instructed to make it clear once again, as he said his government had already done, that Soviet assistance to Cuba, and I quote, "pursued solely the purpose of contributing to the defense capabilities of Cuba," that, and I quote him, "training by Soviet specialists of Cuban nationals in handling defensive armaments was by no means offensive, and if it were otherwise," Mr. Gromyko went on, "the Soviet Government would never become involved in rendering such assistance." That statement also was false.

Neither the United States of America nor the world community of nations can tolerate deliberate deception and offensive threats on the part of any nation, large or small. We no longer live in a world where only the actual firing of weapons represents a sufficient challenge to a nation's security to constitute maximum peril. Nuclear weapons are so destructive and ballistic missiles are so swift, that any substantially increased possibility of their use or any sudden change in their deployment may well be regarded as a definite threat to peace.

For many years both the Soviet Union and the United States, recognizing this fact, have deployed strategic nuclear weapons with great care, never upsetting the precarious status quo which insured that these weapons would not be used in the absence of some vital challenge. Our own strategic missiles have never been transferred to the territory of any other nation under a cloak of secrecy and deception; and our history—unlike that of the Soviets since the end of World War II—demonstrates that we have no desire to dominate or conquer any other nation or impose our system upon its people. Nevertheless, American citizens have become adjusted to living daily on the Bull's-eye of Soviet missiles located inside the U.S.S.R. or in submarines.

In that sense, missiles in Cuba add to an already clear and present danger—although it should be noted the nations of Latin America have never previously been subjected to a potential nuclear threat.

But this secret, swift, and extraordinary buildup of Communist missiles—in an area well known to have a special and historical relationship to the United States and the nations of the Western Hemisphere, in violation of Soviet assurances, and in defiance of American and hemispheric policy—this sudden, clandestine decision to station strategic weapons for the first time outside of Soviet soil—is a deliberately provocative and unjustified change in the status quo which cannot be accepted by this country, if our courage and our commitments are ever to be trusted again by either friend or foe.

The 1930's taught us a clear lesson: aggressive conduct, if allowed to go unchecked and unchallenged ultimately leads to war. This nation is opposed to war. We are also true to our word. Our unswerving objective, therefore, must be to prevent the use of these missiles against this or any other country, and to secure their withdrawal or elimination from the Western Hemisphere.

Our policy has been one of patience and restraint, as befits a peaceful and powerful nation, which leads a worldwide alliance. We have been determined not to be diverted from our central concerns by mere irritants and fanatics. But now further action is required—and it is under way; and these actions may only be the beginning. We will not prematurely or unnecessarily risk the costs of worldwide nuclear war in which even the fruits of victory would be ashes in our mouth—but neither will we shrink from that risk at any time it must be faced.

Acting, therefore, in the defense of our own security and of the entire Western Hemisphere, and under the authority entrusted to me by the Constitution as endorsed by the resolution of the Congress, I have directed that the following initial steps be taken immediately:

First: To halt this offensive buildup, a strict quarantine on all offensive military equipment under shipment to Cuba is being initiated. All ships of any kind bound for Cuba from whatever nation or port will, if found to contain cargoes of offensive weapons, be turned back. This quarantine will be extended, if needed, to other types of cargo and carriers. We are not at this time, however, denying the necessities of life as the Soviets attempted to do in their Berlin blockade of 1948.

Second: I have directed the continued and increased close surveillance of Cuba and its military buildup. The foreign ministers of the OAS, in their communique of October 6, rejected secrecy in such matters in this hemisphere. Should these offensive military preparations continue, thus increasing the threat to the hemisphere, further action will be justified. I have directed the Armed Forces to prepare for any eventualities; and I trust that in the interest of both the Cuban people and the Soviet technicians at the sites, the hazards to all concerned in continuing this threat will be recognized.

Third: It shall be the policy of this Nation to regard any nuclear missile launched from Cuba against any nation in the Western Hemisphere as an attack by the Soviet Union on the United States, requiring a full retaliatory response upon the Soviet Union.

Fourth: As a necessary military precaution, I have reinforced our base at Guantanamo, evacuated today the dependents of our personnel there, and ordered additional military units to be on a standby alert basis.

Fifth: We are calling tonight for an immediate meeting of the Organ of Consultation under the Organization of American States, to consider this threat to hemispheric security and to invoke articles 6 and 8 of the Rio Treaty in support of all necessary action. The United Nations Charter allows for regional security arrangements—and the nations of this hemisphere decided long ago against the military presence of outside powers. Our other allies around the world have also been alerted.

Sixth: Under the Charter of the United Nations, we are asking tonight that an emergency meeting of the Security Council be convoked without delay to take action against this latest Soviet threat to world peace. Our resolution will call for the prompt dismantling and withdrawal of all offensive weapons in Cuba, under the supervision of U.N. observers, before the quarantine can be lifted.

Seventh and finally: I call upon Chairman Khrushchev to halt and eliminate this clandestine, reckless and provocative threat to world peace and to stable relations between our two nations. I call upon him further to abandon this course of world domination, and to join in an historic effort to end the perilous arms race and to transform the history of man. He has an opportunity now to move the world back from the abyss of destruction—by returning to his government's own words that it had no need to station missiles outside its own territory, and withdrawing these weapons from Cuba—by refraining from any action which will widen or deepen the present crisis—and then by participating in a search for peaceful and permanent solutions.

This Nation is prepared to present its case against the Soviet threat to peace, and our own proposals for a peaceful world, at any time and in any forum—in the OAS, in the United Nations, or in any other meeting that could be useful—without limiting our freedom of action. We have in the past made strenuous efforts to limit the spread of nuclear weapons. We have proposed the elimination of all arms and military bases in a fair and effective disarmament treaty. We are prepared to discuss new proposals for the removal of tensions on both sides—including the possibility of a genuinely independent Cuba, free to determine its own destiny. We have no wish to war with the Soviet Union—for we are a peaceful people who desire to live in peace with all other peoples.

But it is difficult to settle or even discuss these problems in an atmosphere of intimidation. That is why this latest Soviet threat—or any other threat which is made either independently or in response to our actions this week—must and will be met with determination. Any hostile move anywhere in the world against the safety and freedom of peoples to whom we are committed—including in particular the brave people of West Berlin—will be met by whatever action is needed.

Finally, I want to say a few words to the captive people of Cuba, to whom this speech is being directly carried by special radio facilities. I speak to you as a friend, as one who knows of your deep attachment to your fatherland, as one who shares your aspirations for liberty and justice for all. And I have watched and the American people have watched with deep sorrow how your nationalist revolution was betrayed—and how your fatherland fell under foreign domination. Now your leaders are no longer Cuban leaders inspired by Cuban ideals. They are puppets and agents of an international conspiracy which has turned Cuba against your friends and neighbors in the Americas—and turned it into the first Latin American country to become a target for nuclear war—the first Latin American country to have these weapons on its soil.

These new weapons are not in your interest. They contribute nothing to your peace and well-being. They can only undermine it. But this country has no wish to cause you to suffer or to impose any system upon you. We know that your lives and land are being used as pawns by those who deny your freedom.

Many times in the past, the Cuban people have risen to throw out tyrants who destroyed their liberty. And I have no doubt that most Cubans today look forward to the time when they will be truly free—free from foreign domination, free to choose their own leaders, free to select their own system, free to own their own land, free to speak and write and worship without fear or degradation. And then shall Cuba be welcomed back to the society of free nations and to the associations of this hemisphere.

My fellow citizens: let no one doubt that this is a difficult and dangerous effort on which we have set out. No one can see precisely what course it will take or what costs or casualties will be incurred. Many months of sacrifice and self-discipline lie ahead—months in which our patience and our will will be tested—months in which many threats and denunciations will keep us aware of our dangers. But the greatest danger of all would be to do nothing.

The path we have chosen for the present is full of hazards, as all paths are—but it is the one most consistent with our character and courage as a nation and our commitments around the world. The cost of freedom is always high—and Americans have always paid it. And one path we shall never choose, and that is the path of surrender or submission.

Our goal is not the victory of might, but the vindication of right—
not peace at the expense of freedom, but both peace and freedom, here
in this hemisphere, and, we hope, around the world. God willing, that
goal will be achieved.

Thank you and good night.

DOCUMENT: COMMENCEMENT ADDRESS AT AMERICAN UNIVERSITY IN WASHINGTON

Date: June 10, 1963

Significance: This speech is notable for Kennedy's call for peaceful
coexistence between the United States and the Soviet Union as he
noted the common humanity of the American and Soviet peoples. The
American University speech would be cited later during the Cold War
as a turning point, marking a more normalized relationship between
the two superpowers.

Source: *Public Papers of the Presidents of the United States: John F.
Kennedy* (Washington, DC: Government Printing Office, 1964),
pp. 459–464.

President Anderson, members of the faculty, board of trustees, distinguished guests, my old colleague, Senator Bob Byrd, who has earned
his degree through many years of attending night law school, while I am
earning mine in the next 30 minutes, distinguished guests, ladies and
gentlemen:

It is with great pride that I participate in this ceremony of the American University, sponsored by the Methodist Church, founded by Bishop
John Fletcher Hurst, and first opened by President Woodrow Wilson in
1914. This is a young and growing university, but it has already fulfilled
Bishop Hurst's enlightened hope for the study of history and public affairs in a city devoted to the making of history and the conduct of the
public's business. By sponsoring this institution of higher learning for
all who wish to learn, whatever their color or their creed, the Methodists
of this area and the Nation deserve the Nation's thanks, and I commend
all those who are today graduating.

Professor Woodrow Wilson once said that every man sent out from
a university should be a man of his nation as well as a man of his time,
and I am confident that the men and women who carry the honor of

graduating from this institution will continue to give from their lives, from their talents, a high measure of public service and public support.

"There are few earthly things more beautiful than a university," wrote John Masefield in his tribute to English universities—and his words are equally true today. He did not refer to spires and towers, to campus greens and ivied walls. He admired the splendid beauty of the university, he said, because it was "a place where those who hate ignorance may strive to know, where those who perceive truth may strive to make others see."

I have, therefore, chosen this time and this place to discuss a topic on which ignorance too often abounds and the truth is too rarely perceived—yet it is the most important topic on earth: world peace.

What kind of peace do I mean? What kind of peace do we seek? Not a Pax Americana enforced on the world by American weapons of war. Not the peace of the grave or the security of the slave. I am talking about genuine peace, the kind of peace that makes life on earth worth living, the kind that enables men and nations to grow and to hope and to build a better life for their children—not merely peace for Americans but peace for all men and women—not merely peace in our time but peace for all time.

I speak of peace because of the new face of war. Total war makes no sense in an age when great powers can maintain large and relatively invulnerable nuclear forces and refuse to surrender without resort to those forces. It makes no sense in an age when a single nuclear weapon contains almost ten times the explosive force delivered by all the allied air forces in the Second World War. It makes no sense in an age when the deadly poisons produced by a nuclear exchange would be carried by wind and water and soil and seed to the far corners of the globe and to generations yet unborn.

Today the expenditure of billions of dollars every year on weapons acquired for the purpose of making sure we never need to use them is essential to keeping the peace. But surely the acquisition of such idle stockpiles—which can only destroy and never create—is not the only, much less the most efficient, means of assuring peace.

I speak of peace, therefore, as the necessary rational end of rational men. I realize that the pursuit of peace is not as dramatic as the pursuit of war—and frequently the words of the pursuer fall on deaf ears. But we have no more urgent task.

Some say that it is useless to speak of world peace or world law or world disarmament—and that it will be useless until the leaders of the Soviet Union adopt a more enlightened attitude. I hope they do. I believe we can help them do it. But I also believe that we must reexamine our own attitude—as individuals and as a Nation—for our attitude is as essential as theirs. And every graduate of this school, every thoughtful citizen who despairs of war and wishes to bring peace, should begin by looking inward—by examining his own attitude toward the possibilities of peace, toward the Soviet Union, toward the course of the cold war and toward freedom and peace here at home.

First: Let us examine our attitude toward peace itself. Too many of us think it is impossible. Too many think it unreal. But that is a dangerous, defeatist belief. It leads to the conclusion that war is inevitable—that mankind is doomed—that we are gripped by forces we cannot control.

We need not accept that view. Our problems are manmade—therefore, they can be solved by man. And man can be as big as he wants. No problem of human destiny is beyond human beings. Man's reason and spirit have often solved the seemingly unsolvable—and we believe they can do it again.

I am not referring to the absolute, infinite concept of peace and good will of which some fantasies and fanatics dream. I do not deny the value of hopes and dreams but we merely invite discouragement and incredulity by making that our only and immediate goal.

Let us focus instead on a more practical, more attainable peace—based not on a sudden revolution in human nature but on a gradual evolution in human institutions—on a series of concrete actions and effective agreements which are in the interest of all concerned. There is no single, simple key to this peace—no grand or magic formula to be adopted by one or two powers. Genuine peace must be the product of many nations, the sum of many acts. It must be dynamic, not static, changing to meet the challenge of each new generation. For peace is a process—a way of solving problems.

With such a peace, there will still be quarrels and conflicting interests, as there are within families and nations. World peace, like community peace, does not require that each man love his neighbor—it requires only that they live together in mutual tolerance, submitting their disputes to a just and peaceful settlement. And history teaches us that enmities between nations, as between individuals, do not last forever. However fixed our likes and dislikes may seem, the tide of time and events will often bring surprising changes in the relations between nations and neighbors.

So let us persevere. Peace need not be impracticable, and war need not be inevitable. By defining our goal more clearly, by making it seem more manageable and less remote, we can help all peoples to see it, to draw hope from it, and to move irresistibly toward it.

Second: Let us reexamine our attitude toward the Soviet Union. It is discouraging to think that their leaders may actually believe what their propagandists write. It is discouraging to read a recent authoritative Soviet text on Military Strategy and find, on page after page, wholly baseless and incredible claims—such as the allegation that "American imperialist circles are preparing to unleash different types of wars . . . that there is a very real threat of a preventive war being unleashed by American imperialists against the Soviet Union . . . [and that] the political aims of the American imperialists are to enslave economically and politically the European and other capitalist countries . . . [and] to achieve world domination ... by means of aggressive wars."

Truly, as it was written long ago: "The wicked flee when no man pursueth." Yet it is sad to read these Soviet statements—to realize the extent of the gulf between us. But it is also a warning—a warning to the American people not to fall into the same trap as the Soviets, not to see only a distorted and desperate view of the other side, not to see conflict as inevitable, accommodation as impossible, and communication as nothing more than an exchange of threats.

No government or social system is so evil that its people must be considered as lacking in virtue. As Americans, we find communism profoundly repugnant as a negation of personal freedom and dignity. But we can still hail the Russian people for their many achievements—in science and space, in economic and industrial growth, in culture and in acts of courage.

Among the many traits the peoples of our two countries have in common, none is stronger than our mutual abhorrence of war. Almost unique among the major world powers, we have never been at war with each other. And no nation in the history of battle ever suffered more than the Soviet Union suffered in the course of the Second World War.

At least 20 million lost their lives. Countless millions of homes and farms were burned or sacked. A third of the nation's territory, including nearly two thirds of its industrial base, was turned into a wasteland—a loss equivalent to the devastation of this country east of Chicago.

Today, should total war ever break out again—no matter how—our two countries would become the primary targets. It is an ironic but accurate fact that the two strongest powers are the two in the most danger of devastation. All we have built, all we have worked for, would be destroyed in the first 24 hours. And even in the cold war, which brings burdens and dangers to so many nations, including this Nation's closest allies—our two countries bear the heaviest burdens. For we are both devoting massive sums of money to weapons that could be better devoted to combating ignorance, poverty, and disease. We are both caught up in a vicious and dangerous cycle in which suspicion on one side breeds suspicion on the other, and new weapons beget counterweapons.

In short, both the United States and its allies, and the Soviet Union and its allies, have a mutually deep interest in a just and genuine peace and in halting the arms race. Agreements to this end are in the interests of the Soviet Union as well as ours—and even the most hostile nations can be relied upon to accept and keep those treaty obligations, and only those treaty obligations, which are in their own interest.

So, let us not be blind to our differences—but let us also direct attention to our common interests and to the means by which those differences can be resolved. And if we cannot end now our differences, at least we can help make the world safe for diversity. For, in the final analysis, our most basic common link is that we all inhabit this small planet. We all breathe the same air. We all cherish our children's future. And we are all mortal.

Third: Let us reexamine our attitude toward the cold war, remembering that we are not engaged in a debate, seeking to pile up debating points. We are not here distributing blame or pointing the finger of judgment. We must deal with the world as it is, and not as it might have been had the history of the last 18 years been different.

We must, therefore, persevere in the search for peace in the hope that constructive changes within the Communist bloc might bring within reach solutions which now seem beyond us. We must conduct our affairs in such a way that it becomes in the Communists' interest to agree on a genuine peace. Above all, while defending our own vital interests, nuclear powers must avert those confrontations which bring an adversary to a choice of either a humiliating retreat or a nuclear war. To adopt that kind of course in the nuclear age would be evidence only of the bankruptcy of our policy—or of a collective death-wish for the world.

To secure these ends, America's weapons are nonprovocative, carefully controlled, designed to deter, and capable of selective use. Our military forces are committed to peace and disciplined in self-restraint. Our diplomats are instructed to avoid unnecessary irritants and purely rhetorical hostility.

For we can seek a relaxation of tension without relaxing our guard. And, for our part, we do not need to use threats to prove that we are resolute. We do not need to jam foreign broadcasts out of fear our faith will be eroded. We are unwilling to impose our system on any unwilling people—but we are willing and able to engage in peaceful competition with any people on earth.

Meanwhile, we seek to strengthen the United Nations, to help solve its financial problems, to make it a more effective instrument for peace, to develop it into a genuine world security system—a system capable of resolving disputes on the basis of law, of insuring the security of the large and the small, and of creating conditions under which arms can finally be abolished.

At the same time we seek to keep peace inside the non-Communist world, where many nations, all of them our friends, are divided over issues which weaken Western unity, which invite Communist intervention or which threaten to erupt into war. Our efforts in West New Guinea, in the Congo, in the Middle East, and in the Indian subcontinent, have been persistent and patient despite criticism from both sides. We have also tried to set an example for others—by seeking to adjust small but significant differences with our own closest neighbors in Mexico and in Canada.

Speaking of other nations, I wish to make one point clear. We are bound to many nations by alliances. Those alliances exist because our concern and theirs substantially overlap. Our commitment to defend Western Europe and West Berlin, for example, stands undiminished because of the identity of our vital interests. The United States will make no deal with the Soviet Union at the expense of other nations and other peoples, not merely because they are our partners, but also because their interests and ours converge.

Our interests converge, however, not only in defending the frontiers of freedom, but in pursuing the paths of peace. It is our hope—and the purpose of allied policies—to convince the Soviet Union that she, too, should let each nation choose its own future, so long as that choice does not interfere with the choices of others. The Communist drive to impose their political and economic system on others is the primary cause of world tension today. For there can be no doubt that, if all nations could refrain from interfering in the self-determination of others, the peace would be much more assured.

This will require a new effort to achieve world law—a new context for world discussions. It will require increased understanding between the Soviets and ourselves. And increased understanding will require increased contact and communication. One step in this direction is the proposed arrangement for a direct line between Moscow and Washington, to avoid on each side the dangerous delays, misunderstandings, and misreadings of the other's actions which might occur at a time of crisis.

We have also been talking in Geneva about the other first-step measures of arms control designed to limit the intensity of the arms race and to reduce the risks of accidental war. Our primary long range interest in Geneva, however, is general and complete disarmament—designed to take place by stages, permitting parallel political developments to build the new institutions of peace which would take the place of arms. The pursuit of disarmament has been an effort of this Government since the 1920's. It has been urgently sought by the past three administrations. And however dim the prospects may be today, we intend to continue this effort—to continue it in order that all countries, including our own, can better grasp what the problems and possibilities of disarmament are.

The one major area of these negotiations where the end is in sight, yet where a fresh start is badly needed, is in a treaty to outlaw nuclear tests. The conclusion of such a treaty, so near and yet so far, would check the spiraling arms race in one of its most dangerous areas. It would place the nuclear powers in a position to deal more effectively with one of the greatest hazards which man faces in 1963, the further spread of nuclear arms. It would increase our security—it would decrease the prospects of war. Surely this goal is sufficiently important to require our steady pursuit, yielding neither to the temptation to give up the whole effort nor the temptation to give up our insistence on vital and responsible safeguards.

I am taking this opportunity, therefore, to announce two important decisions in this regard.

First: Chairman Khrushchev, Prime Minister Macmillan, and I have agreed that high-level discussions will shortly begin in Moscow looking toward early agreement on a comprehensive test ban treaty. Our hopes must be tempered with the caution of history—but with our hopes go the hopes of all mankind.

Second: To make clear our good faith and solemn convictions on the matter, I now declare that the United States does not propose to conduct nuclear tests in the atmosphere so long as other states do not do so. We will not be the first to resume. Such a declaration is no substitute for a formal binding treaty, but I hope it will help us achieve one. Nor would such a treaty be a substitute for disarmament, but I hope it will help us achieve it.

Finally, my fellow Americans, let us examine our attitude toward peace and freedom here at home. The quality and spirit of our own society must justify and support our efforts abroad. We must show it in the dedication of our own lives—as many of you who are graduating today will have a unique opportunity to do, by serving without pay in the Peace Corps abroad or in the proposed National Service Corps here at home.

But wherever we are, we must all, in our daily lives, live up to the age-old faith that peace and freedom walk together. In too many of our cities today, the peace is not secure because the freedom is incomplete.

It is the responsibility of the executive branch at all levels of government—local, State, and National—to provide and protect that freedom for all of our citizens by all means within their authority. It is the responsibility of the legislative branch at all levels, wherever that authority is not now adequate, to make it adequate. And it is the responsibility of all citizens in all sections of this country to respect the rights of all others and to respect the law of the land.

All this is not unrelated to world peace. "When a man's ways please the Lord," the Scriptures tell us, "he maketh even his enemies to be at peace with him." And is not peace, in the last analysis, basically a matter of human rights—the right to live out our lives without fear of devastation—the right to breathe air as nature provided it—the right of future generations to a healthy existence?

While we proceed to safeguard our national interests, let us also safeguard human interests. And the elimination of war and arms is clearly in the interest of both. No treaty, however much it may be to the advantage of all, however tightly it may be worded, can provide absolute security against the risks of deception and evasion. But it can—if it is sufficiently effective in its enforcement and if it is sufficiently in the interests of its signers—offer far more security and far fewer risks than an unabated, uncontrolled, unpredictable arms race.

The United States, as the world knows, will never start a war. We do not want a war. We do not now expect a war. This generation of Americans has already had enough—more than enough—of war and hate and oppression. We shall be prepared if others wish it. We shall be alert to try to stop it. But we shall also do our part to build a world of peace where the weak are safe and the strong are just. We are not helpless before that task or hopeless of its success. Confident and unafraid, we labor on—not toward a strategy of annihilation but toward a strategy of peace.

DOCUMENT: ADDRESS TO THE NATION ON CIVIL RIGHTS

Date: June 11, 1963

Significance: This speech is the first time that an American president addressed civil rights and equality for African Americans in moral terms. In his remarks, President Kennedy also called for a comprehensive civil rights bill that became law when President Lyndon B. Johnson signed the measure into law in 1964; this ended racial segregation in the South.

Source: *Public Papers of the Presidents of the United States: John F. Kennedy* (Washington, DC: Government Printing Office, 1964), pp. 468–470.

Good evening my fellow citizens:

This afternoon, following a series of threats and defiant statements, the presence of Alabama National Guardsmen was required on the University of Alabama to carry out the final and unequivocal order of the United States District Court of the Northern District of Alabama. That order called for the admission of two clearly qualified young Alabama residents who happened to have been born Negro.

That they were admitted peacefully on the campus is due in good measure to the conduct of the students of the University of Alabama, who met their responsibilities in a constructive way.

I hope that every American, regardless of where he lives, will stop and examine his conscience about this and other related incidents. This Nation was founded by men of many nations and backgrounds. It was founded on the principle that all men are created equal, and that the rights of every man are diminished when the rights of one man are threatened.

Today we are committed to a worldwide struggle to promote and protect the rights of all who wish to be free. And when Americans are sent to Viet-Nam or West Berlin, we do not ask for whites only. It ought to be possible, therefore, for American students of any color to attend any public institution they select without having to be backed up by troops.

It ought to be possible for American consumers of any color to receive equal service in places of public accommodation, such as hotels and restaurants and theaters and retail stores, without being forced to resort to demonstrations in the street, and it ought to be possible for American citizens of any color to register to vote in a free election without interference or fear of reprisal.

It ought to be possible, in short, for every American to enjoy the privileges of being American without regard to his race or his color. In short, every American ought to have the right to be treated as he would wish to be treated, as one would wish his children to be treated. But this is not the case.

The Negro baby born in America today, regardless of the section of the Nation in which he is born, has about one-half as much chance of completing high school as a white baby born in the same place on the same day, one-third as much chance of completing college, one-third as much chance of becoming a professional man, twice as much chance of becoming unemployed, about one-seventh as much chance of earning $10,000 a year, a life expectancy which is 7 years shorter, and the prospects of earning only half as much.

This is not a sectional issue. Difficulties over segregation and discrimination exist in every city, in every State of the Union, producing in many cities a rising tide of discontent that threatens the public safety. Nor is this a partisan issue. In a time of domestic crisis men of good will and generosity should be able to unite regardless of party or politics. This is not even a legal or legislative issue alone. It is better to settle these matters in the courts than on the streets, and new laws are needed at every level, but law alone cannot make men see right.

We are confronted primarily with a moral issue. It is as old as the scriptures and is as clear as the American Constitution.

The heart of the question is whether all Americans are to be afforded equal rights and equal opportunities, whether we are going to treat our fellow Americans as we want to be treated. If an American, because his skin is dark, cannot eat lunch in a restaurant open to the public, if he cannot send his children to the best public school available, if he cannot vote for the public officials who will represent him, if, in short, he cannot enjoy the full and free life which all of us want, then who among us would be content to have the color of his skin changed and stand in his place? Who among us would then be content with the counsels of patience and delay?

One hundred years of delay have passed since President Lincoln freed the slaves, yet their heirs, their grandsons, are not fully free. They are not yet freed from the bonds of injustice. They are not yet freed from social and economic oppression. And this Nation, for all its hopes and all its boasts, will not be fully free until all its citizens are free.

We preach freedom around the world, and we mean it, and we cherish our freedom here at home, but are we to say to the world, and much more importantly, to each other that this is the land of the free except for the Negroes; that we have no second-class citizens except Negroes; that we have no class or caste system, no ghettos, no master race except with respect to Negroes?

Now the time has come for this Nation to fulfill its promise. The events in Birmingham and elsewhere have so increased the cries for equality that no city or State or legislative body can prudently choose to ignore them.

The fires of frustration and discord are burning in every city, North and South, where legal remedies are not at hand. Redress is sought in the streets, in demonstrations, parades, and protests which create tensions and threaten violence and threaten lives.

We face, therefore, a moral crisis as a country and as a people. It cannot be met by repressive police action. It cannot be left to increased demonstrations in the streets. It cannot be quieted by token moves or talk. It is time to act in the Congress, in your State and local legislative body and, above all, in all of our daily lives.

It is not enough to pin the blame on others, to say this is a problem of one section of the country or another, or deplore the facts that we face. A great change is at hand, and our task, our obligation, is to make that revolution, that change, peaceful and constructive for all.

Those who do nothing are inviting shame as well as violence. Those who act boldly are recognizing right as well as reality.

Next week I shall ask the Congress of the United States to act, to make a commitment it has not fully made in this century to the proposition that race has no place in American life or law. The Federal judiciary has upheld that proposition in the conduct of its affairs, including the employment of Federal personnel, the use of Federal facilities, and the sale of federally financed housing.

But there are other necessary measures which only the Congress can provide, and they must be provided at this session. The old code of equity law under which we live commands for every wrong a remedy, but in too many communities, in too many parts of the country, wrongs are inflicted on Negro citizens and there are no remedies at law. Unless the Congress acts, their only remedy is in the street.

I am, therefore, asking the Congress to enact legislation giving all Americans the right to be served in facilities which are open to the public—hotels, restaurants, theaters, retail stores, and similar establishments.

This seems to me to be an elementary right. Its denial is an arbitrary indignity that no American in 1963 should have to endure, but many do.

I have recently met with scores of business leaders urging them to take voluntary action to end this discrimination and I have been encouraged by their response, and in the last 2 weeks over 75 cities have seen progress made in desegregating these kinds of facilities. But many are unwilling to act alone, and for this reason, nationwide legislation is needed if we are to move this problem from the streets to the courts.

I am also asking the Congress to authorize the Federal Government to participate more fully in lawsuits designed to end segregation in public education. We have succeeded in persuading many districts to desegregate voluntarily. Dozens have admitted Negroes without violence. Today a Negro is attending a State-supported institution in every one of our 50 States, but the pace is very slow.

Too many Negro children entering segregated grade schools at the time of the Supreme Court's decision 9 years ago will enter segregated high schools this fall, having suffered a loss which can never be restored. The lack of an adequate education denies the Negro a chance to get a decent job.

The orderly implementation of the Supreme Court decision, therefore, cannot be left solely to those who may not have the economic resources to carry the legal action or who may be subject to harassment.

Other features will also be requested, including greater protection for the right to vote. But legislation, I repeat, cannot solve this problem alone. It must be solved in the homes of every American in every community across our country.

In this respect I want to pay tribute to those citizens North and South who have been working in their communities to make life better for all. They are acting not out of a sense of legal duty but out of a sense of human decency.

Like our soldiers and sailors in all parts of the world they are meeting freedom's challenge on the firing line, and I salute them for their honor and their courage.

My fellow Americans, this is a problem which faces us all—in every city of the North as well as the South. Today there are Negroes unemployed, two or three times as many compared to whites, inadequate in education, moving into the large cities, unable to find work, young people particularly out of work without hope, denied equal rights, denied the opportunity to eat at a restaurant or lunch counter or go to a movie theater, denied the right to a decent education, denied almost today the right to attend a State university even though qualified. It seems to me that these are matters which concern us all, not merely Presidents or Congressmen or Governors, but every citizen of the United States.

This is one country. It has become one country because all of us and all the people who came here had an equal chance to develop their talents.

We cannot say to 10 percent of the population that you can't have that right; that your children cannot have the chance to develop whatever talents they have; that the only way that they are going to get their rights is to go into the streets and demonstrate. I think we owe them and we owe ourselves a better country than that.

Therefore, I am asking for your help in making it easier for us to move ahead and to provide the kind of equality of treatment which we would want ourselves; to give a chance for every child to be educated to the limit of his talents.

As I have said before, not every child has an equal talent or an equal ability or an equal motivation, but they should have an equal right to develop their talent and their ability and their motivation, to make something of themselves.

We have a right to expect that the Negro community will be responsible, will uphold the law, but they have a right to expect that the law will be fair, that the Constitution will be color blind, as Justice Harlan said at the turn of the century.

This is what we are talking about and this is a matter which concerns this country and what it stands for, and in meeting it I ask the support of all our citizens.

Thank you very much.

DOCUMENT: REMARKS IN THE RUDOLPH WILDE PLATZ, BERLIN ("ICH BIN EIN BERLINER.")

Date: June 26, 1963

Significance: This speech was delivered to a large crowd in West Berlin and was meant to reassure West Berliners of the American commitment to defend the city. Following the Berlin Crisis of 1961 and the Cuban Missile Crisis of 1962, the words of Kennedy's speech were cited not just during and immediately after his remarks but served as a rallying point for the remainder of the Cold War.

Source: *Public Papers of the Presidents of the United States: John F. Kennedy* (Washington, DC: Government Printing Office, 1964), pp. 524–525.

I am proud to come to this city as the guest of your distinguished Mayor, who has symbolized throughout the world the fighting spirit of West Berlin. And I am proud to visit the Federal Republic with your distinguished Chancellor who for so many years has committed Germany to democracy and freedom and progress, and to come here in the company of my fellow American, General Clay, who has been in this city during its great moments of crisis and will come again if ever needed.

Two thousand years ago the proudest boast was "civis Romanus sum." Today, in the world of freedom, the proudest boast is "Ich bin ein Berliner."

I appreciate my interpreter translating my German!

There are many people in the world who really don't understand, or say they don't, what is the great issue between the free world and the Communist world. Let them come to Berlin. There are some who say that communism is the wave of the future. Let them come to Berlin. And there are some who say in Europe and elsewhere we can work with the Communists. Let them come to Berlin. And there are even a few who say that it is true that communism is an evil system, but it permits us to make economic progress. Lass' sie nach Berlin kommen. Let them come to Berlin.

Freedom has many difficulties and democracy is not perfect, but we have never had to put a wall up to keep our people in, to prevent them from leaving us. I want to say, on behalf of my countrymen, who live many miles away on the other side of the Atlantic, who are far distant from you, that they take the greatest pride that they have been able to share with you, even from a distance, the story of the last 18 years. I know of no town, no city, that has been besieged for 18 years that still lives with the vitality and the force, and the hope and the determination of the city of West Berlin. While the wall is the most obvious and vivid demonstration of the failures of the Communist system, for all the world to see, we take no satisfaction in it, for it is, as your Mayor has said, an offense not only against history but an offense against humanity, separating families, dividing husbands and wives and brothers and sisters, and dividing a people who wish to be joined together.

What is true of this city is true of Germany—real, lasting peace in Europe can never be assured as long as one German out of four is denied the elementary right of free men, and that is to make a free choice. In 18 years of peace and good faith, this generation of Germans has earned the right to be free, including the right to unite their families and their nation in lasting peace, with good will to all people. You live in a defended island of freedom, but your life is part of the main. So let me ask you as I close, to lift your eyes beyond the dangers of today, to the hopes of tomorrow, beyond the freedom merely of this city of Berlin, or your country of Germany, to the advance of freedom everywhere, beyond the wall to the day of peace with justice, beyond yourselves and ourselves to all mankind.

Freedom is indivisible, and when one man is enslaved, all are not free. When all are free, then we can look forward to that day when this city will be joined as one and this country and this great Continent of Europe in a peaceful and hopeful globe. When that day finally comes, as it will, the people of West Berlin can take sober satisfaction in the fact that they were in the front lines for almost two decades.

All free men, wherever they may live, are citizens of Berlin, and, therefore, as a free man, I take pride in the words "Ich bin ein Berliner."

SELECTED ANNOTATED BIBLIOGRAPHY

PRIMARY SOURCES

The most important collection of primary sources on the life of John F. Kennedy is housed in the John Fitzgerald Kennedy Library in Boston, although there is little of his personal correspondence there and some of the material remains closed to researchers for security reasons or because of donor restrictions. Nonetheless, there is an abundance of public papers for his congressional and senatorial years as well as his slightly more than 1,000 days as president. Some of the most valuable information is in the more than 1,000 oral history interviews, some of which are available online at the library's website. The National Archives in Washington, DC, includes the John F. Kennedy Assassination Records Collection, with material from the CIA and FBI as well as the Warren Commission and the House Select Committee on Assassinations. Kennedy's speeches and public statements have been published in *Public Papers of the Presidents of the United States: John F. Kennedy, Containing the Public Messages, Speeches, and Statements of the President, 1961–1963*, 3 vols. (Washington, DC: Government Printing Office, 1962–1964). Also helpful is *John Fitzgerald Kennedy: A Compilation of*

Statements and Speeches Made during His Service in the United States Senate and House of Representatives (Washington, DC: Government Printing Office, 1964) and John F. Kennedy, *Freedom of Communications, Part One: The Speeches, Remarks, Press Conferences and Statements of Senator John F. Kennedy, August 1 through November 7, 1960* (Washington, DC: Government Printing Office, 1961).

President Kennedy taped many conversations, and there are two important transcriptions of recorded conversations on key developments during the Kennedy presidency. One can follow the deliberations during the Cuban Missile Crisis in Ernest R. May and Philip D. Zelikow, eds., *The Kennedy Tapes: Inside the White House during the Cuban Missile Crisis* (Cambridge, MA: Belknap Press of Harvard University Press, 1997). Oval Office discussions about the civil rights struggle can be followed in Jonathan Rosenberg and Zachary Karabell, *Kennedy, Johnson, and the Quest for Justice: The Civil Rights Tapes* (New York: W. W. Norton, 2003). Finally, two books by Kennedy help explain his political philosophy: *Why England Slept* (1940; repr., Westport, CT: Greenwood Press, 1981) and *Profiles in Courage* (1956; reissue, New York: Harper-Collins, 2003).

NEWSPAPER ARTICLES

An excellent source of the coverage of Kennedy's life and presidency is the *New York Times*, which is available in an historical database. Articles useful in this study include:

"Cuba Action Gets Public's Backing." *New York Times*. October 23, 1962, p. 21.

"Excerpts from the Testimony of Robert Kennedy before Senate Panel." *New York Times*. January 14, 1961, p. 8.

"Kennedy's Son Is Hero in Pacific as Destroyer Splits His PT Boat." *New York Times*. August 20, 1943, p. 1.

"Kennedy Urges Arms Cut Drive." *New York Times*. August 15, 1958, p. 2.

Lehmann-Haupt, Christopher. "Kennedy Assassination Answers." *New York Times*. September 9, 1993, p. C18.

Morris, John D. "Johnson Names a 7-Man Panel to Investigate Assassination." *New York Times*. November 30, 1963, p. 1.

Oshinsky, David. "In the Heart of Conspiracy." *New York Times*. January 27, 2008, http://www.nytimes.com/2008/01/27/review/Oshinsky-t.html (accessed March 22, 2010).

Phillips, Cabell. "Case History of a Senate Race." *New York Times Sunday Magazine*. October 26, 1952, pp. SM 10–11 and 49–51.

Phillips, Cabell. "Johnson Pledges Facts in Killings." *New York Times*. November 26, 1963, p. 15.

"Protestant Groups' Statements." *New York Times*. September 8, 1960, p. 25.

Weiner, Tim. "A Blast at Secrecy in Kennedy Killing." *New York Times*. September 29, 1998, p. A17.

AUTOBIOGRAPHIES

There are several autobiographies by members of the Kennedy family, friends, and individuals who worked on Kennedy's staffs in Congress, the Senate, and the White House that are helpful in assessing Kennedy.

Kennedy, Edward M. *True Compass: A Memoir*. New York: Twelve, 2009.

Kennedy, Rose Fitzgerald. *Times to Remember*. Garden City, NY: Doubleday, 1974.

Lincoln, Evelyn. *My Twelve Years with John F. Kennedy*. New York: David McKay, 1965.

O'Brien, Lawrence F. *No Final Victories: A Life in Politics from John F. Kennedy to Watergate*. Garden City, NY: Doubleday, 1974.

O'Donnell, Kenneth P., and David F. Powers with Joe McCarthy. *"Johnny, We Hardly Knew Ye": Memories of John Fitzgerald Kennedy*. Boston: Little, Brown, 1970.

O'Neill, Tip, with William Novak. *Man of the House: The Life and Political Memoirs of Speaker Tip O'Neill*. New York: Random House, 1987.

Schlesinger, Arthur, Jr. *Journals, 1952–2000*. New York: Penguin Press, 2007.

Sorensen, Theodore C. *Counselor: A Life at the Edge of History*. New York: HarperCollins, 2008.

Thompson, Kenneth W. *The Kennedy Presidency: Seventeen Intimate Perspectives of John F. Kennedy*. Lanham, MD: University Press of America, 1985.

Wofford, Harris. *Of Kennedys and Kings: Making Sense of the Sixties*. New York: Farrar, Straus & Giroux, 1980.

JOURNAL ARTICLES

Some of the best work done on specialized topics in the life of Kennedy can be found in magazines and academic journals. Articles useful in this study include:

Giglio, James N. "Growing Up Kennedy: The Role of Medical Ailments in the Life of JFK, 1920–1957." *Journal of Family History* 31 (October 2006): 358–385.

Jeffries, John W. "The Quest for National Purpose of 1960." *American Quarterly* 30 (Autumn 1978): 455–470.

BIOGRAPHIES

There are a number of excellent full-length biographies of John Kennedy. In particular, five are worthy of attention.

Collier, Peter, and David Horowitz. *The Kennedys*. London: Pan Books, 1984.

Dallek, Robert. *An Unfinished Life: John F. Kennedy, 1917–1963*. New York: Back Bay Books, 2003.

O'Brien, Michael. *John Kennedy: A Biography*. New York: Thomas Dunne Books, 2005.

Parmet, Herbert S. *Jack: The Struggles of John F. Kennedy* (New York: Dial Press, 1980).

Parmet, Herbert S. *JFK: The Presidency of John F. Kennedy* (New York: Dial Press, 1983).

There are a couple of helpful studies of Kennedy's early years:

Blair, Joan, and Clay Blair Jr. *The Search for JFK*. New York: Berkley Medallion Books, 1976.

Hamilton, Nigel. *JFK: Reckless Youth*. New York: Random House, 1992.

Among the biographies of Robert Kennedy, Evan Thomas's is the best.

Thomas, Evan. *Robert Kennedy: His Life*. New York: Simon & Schuster, 2002.

Over time, scholars and political commentators have published critical studies of Kennedy's life. Several stand out as important works that have contributed to a revision of the image this generation has of him, particularly his personal behavior.

Fairlie, Henry. *The Kennedy Promise: The Politics of Expectation*. Garden City, NY: Doubleday, 1973.

Hersh, Seymour M. *The Dark Side of Camelot*. Boston: Little, Brown, 1997.

Miroff, Bruce. *Pragmatic Illusions: The Presidential Politics of John F. Kennedy*. New York: David McKay, 1976.

Reeves, Thomas C. *A Question of Character: A Life of John F. Kennedy*. New York: Free Press, 1991.

Wills, Garry. *The Kennedy Imprisonment: A Meditation on Power*. Boston: Little, Brown, 1982.

STUDIES OF THE KENNEDY PRESIDENCY

Among the large number of studies of Kennedy's years in the White House, the best book is James N. Giglio, *The Presidency of John F. Kennedy*, 2nd ed. (Lawrence: University Press of Kansas, 2006). Other useful works include:

Barber, James David. *The Presidential Character: Predicting Performance in the White House*. 3rd ed. Englewood Cliffs, NJ: Prentice-Hall, 1985.

Bernstein, Irving. *Promises Kept: John F. Kennedy's New Frontier*. New York: Oxford University Press, 1991.

Reeves, Richard. *President Kennedy: Profile of Power*. New York: Touchstone, 1993.

Schlesinger, Arthur, Jr. *A Thousand Days: John F. Kennedy in the White House*. Boston: Houghton Mifflin, 1965.

Sorensen, Theodore C. *Kennedy*. New York: Harper and Row, 1965.

SPECIALIZED STUDIES

There are many books dealing with domestic and foreign policy in the Kennedy administration as well as life in the White House.

Brauer, Carl M. *John F. Kennedy and the Second Reconstruction*. New York: Columbia University Press, 1977.

Herring, George. *America's Longest War: The United States and Vietnam, 1950–1975*. New York: John Wiley, 1979.

Isaacs, Jeremy, and Taylor Downing. *Cold War: An Illustrated History, 1945–1991*. Boston: Little, Brown, 1998.

Preble, Christopher A. *John F. Kennedy and the Missile Gap*. De Kalb: Northern Illinois University Press, 2004.

Rabe, Stephen G. *John F. Kennedy: World Leader*. Washington, DC: Potomac Books, 2010.

Smith, Sally Bedell. *Grace and Power: The Private World of the Kennedy White House*. New York: Random House, 2004.

Spoto, Donald. *Jacqueline Bouvier Kennedy Onassis: A Life*. New York: St. Martin's Press, 2000.

Thomas, Evan. *Robert Kennedy: His Life*. New York: Simon and Schuster, 2000.

STUDIES OF THE KENNEDY ASSASSINATION

There is a plethora of books offering conspiracy theories on the Kennedy assassination. Four studies are important in answering the conspiracy theories and demonstrating the impact the assassination had on the nation.

Blaine, Gerald, with Lisa McCubbin. *The Kennedy Detail: JFK's Secret Service Agents Break Their Silence*. New York: Gallery Books, 2010.

Bugliosi, Vincent. *Reclaiming History: The Assassination of President John F. Kennedy*. New York: W.W. Norton, 2007.

Piereson, James. *Camelot and the Cultural Revolution: How the Assassination of John F. Kennedy Shattered American Liberalism*. New York: Encounter Books, 2009.

Posner, Gerald. *Case Closed: Lee Harvey Oswald and the Assassination of JFK*. New York: Random House, 1993.

INDEX

About the Authors

MICHAEL MEAGHER is Associate Professor of Political Science at Missouri University of Science and Technology, Rolla, Missouri. He is the author of a number of articles on John F. Kennedy and on American political thought.

LARRY D. GRAGG is Curators Professor of History and Chair of the Department of History and Political Science at Missouri University of Science and Technology, Rolla, Missouri. The author of several books on colonial and Revolutionary-era America, he is currently writing two books on the history of Las Vegas, Nevada.